Sara Lewis

This edition is published by Parragon Books Ltd 2015

LOVE FOOD is an imprint of Parragon Books Ltd

Parragon Books Ltd
Chartist House, 15-17 Trim Street
Bath, BA1 1HA UK

www.parragon.com/lovefood

ISBN: 978-1-4748-0402-8

Printed in China

Project managed by Kerry Starr
New recipes and food styling by Sara Lewis
New photography by Haarala Hamilton
Nutritional information by Judith Wills

Notes for the reader
This book uses both metric and imperial measurements. Follow the same units of measurements throughout, do not mix metric and imperial. All spoon measurements are level: teaspoons are assumed to be 5ml and tablespoons 15ml. Unless otherwise stated, milk is assumed to be skimmed, eggs and individual vegetables are medium, pepper is freshly ground black pepper and all root vegetables should be peeled prior to use. Any optional ingredients and seasoning to taste are not included in the nutritional analysis.

While the author has made all reasonable efforts to ensure that the information contained in this book is accurate and up to date at the time of publication, anyone reading this book should note the following important points:-

• Medical and pharmaceutical knowledge is constantly changing and the author and publisher cannot and do not guarantee the accuracy or appropriateness of the contents of this book;

• In any event, this book is not intended to be, and should not be relied upon, as a substitute for appropriate, tailored professional advice. Both the author and publisher strongly recommend that a doctor or other healthcare professional is consulted before embarking on major dietary changes;

• For the reasons set out above, and to the fullest extent permitted by law, the author and the publisher: (i) cannot and do not accept any legal duty of care or responsibility in relation to the accuracy or appropriateness of the contents of this book, even where expressed as 'advice' or using other words to this effect; and (ii) disclaim any liability, loss, damage or risk that may be claimed or incurred as a consequence – directly or indirectly – of the use and/or application of any contents of this book.

The soup bar

Soup is back in fashion and thought by some to be the new juice. Healthy, low in fat, energy boosting and packed with immune boosting vitamins and minerals. But for many, soup has never been off the menu. Most of us will have a memory of a favourite childhood soup that warmed us on a cold wintry day. Soup can also offer a comforting hug in a bowl when studying or working, or as a general pick me up after a tiring day.

Our mothers and grannies knew a good way to stretch the budget when funds were low with their waste not want not mantra. While old-fashioned bone broths have long been known to boost health and recovery, in America bone broths are the new trend in New York and served in place of tea or coffee as a caffeine free health boosting alternative to de-stress busy office workers.

Soups can be as varied as your imagination will allow, from brightly coloured, ultra smooth puréed superfood-packed veggie combos, to rustic spiced energy boosting bean and meat soups, light and fresh tasting summer soups, to body balancing detox specials. Raw, natural ingredients, locally bought, this is home cooking at its easiest and simplest.

Bone broth – the new craze

For centuries, cultures all over the world have made their own bone broths, slowly simmered beef, chicken or veal bones flavoured with herbs and aromatics then strained to make little concentrated cups of goodness. Rich in bone building and strengthening minerals and vitamins plus collagen, these clear broths have long been thought to aid healing, act as an anti-inflammatory, boost the immune system and aid digestion. They also contain glucosamine and chondroitin, two supplements many people take for joint pain relief. As interest in the paleo diet has grown, so too has the consumption of bone broths.

Soup – the healthy option

While we know we should be eating more vegetables and wholegrains, while cutting back on fat, sugar and salt, actually putting it into practice can sometimes feel harder than it should. Making up a batch of soup is quick and easy, leaving it to simmer while you get on with something else. Ladle into a bowl and serve with warm wholewheat bread and you have a delicious wholesome meal that will boost your veggy intake, energy and protein levels without you realizing. The more healthy superfoods you eat, the less room you will have for junk food. Any leftovers can be eaten next day for a speedy lunch, or frozen for another day.

The key to a healthy diet is variety and with such a mix of ingredients that can be added to soups it is easy to include a wide range of essential vitamins, minerals, protein, complex carbohydrates and healthy fats all essential for energy, growth, repair, immunity and essential metabolic processes.

The brighter the colour of the vegetable the better for us they will be. Vegetables are packed with antioxidants and phytochemicals thought to help protect the body against cancer and to boost immunity. Plus essential soluble fibre to help lower cholesterol. Most vegetables are low calorie so portion sizes can be generous.

Fermented vegetables such as the Korean pickle kimchi are also gaining popularity and thought to

aid digestion and absorption of essential nutrients by promoting healthy bacteria in the gut, many of which have been suppressed by a Western diet rich in sugar and junk food. The amount of healthy bacteria made in the stomach also reduces with age and after serious illness so adding a few spoonfuls of fermented vegetables is an easy way to boost the numbers of healthy bacteria. Made with a base of Chinese leaves; radishes, carrots, leeks and ginger may also be added. Eastern European sauerkraut or pickled and fermented cabbage also works in much the same way. Fermented black soy beans, fermented brown or white rice miso is also popular in China, Japan and Korea.

Boost energy levels with slow release carbs found in wholegrains such as brown rice, wholewheat, barley or oat grains, no soak lentils or dried or canned pulses or beans. They also help maintain a healthy digestive system and help to lower blood cholesterol so aiding heart health.

Nuts and seeds add protein, so too can quinoa which is the only plant food to contain all the essential amino acids that make up protein. Although higher in calories than some other foods, nuts and seeds also contain minerals and some contain Omega 3 and 6 essential fatty acids. Grind the nuts and use to thicken soups, or leave whole and lightly toast to garnish soups.

Forget about soups laden with cream or butter; these healthier options can be made with nut milks with no added sweeteners, 0% fat natural yogurt for a fat-free swirl or low fat soft cheese for a creamy tasting boost for a lower calorie alternative. Fry off veggies in a little natural virgin olive oil or rice bran oil to add extra flavour rather than butter.

Quantities of meat and fish can also be reduced when making soup without affecting the taste. An 85 g/3 oz portion of diced casserole beef would be unacceptable as a portion size served separately but added to soup you really don't feel as though you are being short changed.

Taking stock

The secret to making good soups is all about the stock that you use. Stock should be full flavoured and with the exception of vegetable stock, rich with gelatine. Poor stock can turn a promising mix of vegetables into a dull and tasteless soup. Making your own stock takes just a matter of minutes to get started then leave to simmer gently. Meaty stocks are cheap and thrifty to make as they use bones that would otherwise be thrown away. Don't discard that chicken carcass after a roast chicken but simmer with vegetables and herbs then strain and use as a practically free base to the next meal. The same applies for a duck, pheasant or guinea fowl carcass too.

For beef stock, ask your butcher for some marrow bones and brown these in the oven with onions and carrots, even a spoonful of dark brown sugar before transferring to a large saucepan and gently simmering with water. Lamb bones can be quite strong tasting and are best kept for making Scotch broth style soups with mixed root vegetables and grains. A gammon or ham bone can also be used – although do not add extra salt – and is great with split pea or other healthy grain based soups.

What vegetables are best?

Traditionally all stocks are flavoured with a trio of onions, celery and carrots. Peel off the outer onion leaves but leave on the inner brown layers as this will add colour and extra flavour. Keep the best celery sticks for salads or to eat with cheese, but add the leafy tops and the thicker outer stems to the stock. The green leafy tops from leeks also make a flavourful addition, while fennel bulbs add a delicate aniseed

flavour. Carrots add body and help the colour of the stock. Avoid adding turnips as their flavour can be a little bitter after long slow cooking.

Add flavour with herbs

Choose a mix of fresh herbs from the garden, adding rosemary or sage, thyme, parsley and bay leaves for beef or chicken stock, or tarragon, fennel, chives and parsley for fish stock. Traditionally tied with fine string or wrapped in muslin and tied with string for easy removal, you can just add the herb stems to the stock and discard after straining. Dried bought bouquet garni look a little like tea bags and can be used if you don't have growing herbs.

Long and slow

Don't try to hurry cooking. Meat based stocks should never be allowed to boil hard as this will result in a thick muddy looking jelly when cooled instead of a semi clear one. Aim to cover the vegetables and bones by an extra two thirds of cold water, bring slowly to the boil then partly cover with a lid and gently simmer for 4-5 hours for beef bone broth or 1½-2 hours for chicken bone broth. Fish stock is the exception requiring just 30 minutes simmering, any longer and the stock will become bitter.

Fresh stock or stock cubes?

Readymade stock cubes or bouillon powder will never be as good as homemade but certainly make a handy emergency storecupboard standby. Choose those that are low in salt and not too highly flavoured or they will dominate other flavours in the soup. Pick from a range of beef, chicken, lamb, ham, fish and vegetable stock. Always make up with water as the pack directs and if anything, add slightly more water rather than less.

Taste test

After simmering you should have about one third less liquid than you started with. Strain into a jug and taste a little. If the stock tastes thin, return to the saucepan and simmer longer to reduce and concentrate the flavours, especially important for a simple bone broth without extra additions. The longer you simmer the more intense the flavour will become. Very long simmering will reduce the stock down to an almost sticky glaze. If you have reduced more of the liquid down than you had meant to, top up with a little extra water or wine.

To keep the amount of salt in our diet as low as possible, add salt to the finished soup rather than to the stock base. Cut down on fat too by either removing any fat that floats on the top of the strained stock with kitchen paper or cool then chill and scoop off with a spoon. When meaty or fish stocks have been chilled for several hours they will thicken and become almost jelly like.

Stock or broth?

Stock is the base of all soups and known as 'fond' in French, which translates to foundation, and can be made with bones or vegetables. Bone broth is really a more concentrated form of stock that is intensely flavoured and concentrated and can be served as it is without any additional ingredients or finished with other finely diced vegetables or meat or both for a second cooking.

Clearing bone broths

If your finished beef stock isn't quite as clear as you would like it to be then lightly whisk 2 egg whites until frothy in a small bowl. Pour the cold cloudy bone broth or stock into a saucepan, leaving behind any sediment. Gently heat until warm. Add the egg whites and bring slowly to the boil. Simmer for 5 minutes then ladle into a muslin lined sieve set over a bowl or jug. The egg whites will act like a magnet and draw all the impurities into the egg white and then trap them there leaving the rest of the liquid clear.

Vegetable stock

Makes: about 850 ml/1½ pints   Prep: 10 minutes   Cook: 55 minutes

Adapt and vary this recipe to use a mix of vegetables that you have but avoid starchy root vegetables such as potatoes, parsnips or turnips as they will make the stock cloudy.

Time to get started

* 1 tbsp olive oil
* 1 onion, quartered
* 2 carrots, thickly sliced
* 2 celery sticks, thickly sliced
* 1 leek, thickly sliced
* 115 g/4 oz button mushrooms, sliced
* 2 tomatoes, diced
* 1 bouquet garni
* ½ tsp black peppercorns
* 1.2 litres/2 pints cold water

Heat the oil in a medium saucepan, add the onion, carrot, celery and leek and fry gently for 5 minutes until the vegetables are softened but not coloured. Stir in the mushrooms and tomatoes and fry gently for 5 minutes. Tuck in the bouquet garni, sprinkle in the peppercorns and pour in the cold water. Bring just to the boil.

Partly cover and simmer for 45 minutes. Strain through a fine sieve and leave to cool. Refrigerate up to 2 days or freeze up to 3 months.

Chicken stock

Makes: about 850 ml/1½ pints   Prep: 10 minutes   Cook: 1½-2 hours

This is perhaps the easiest and most flavourful of all the stocks to make.

How to make it

* 1 kg/2 lb 4 oz cooked chicken carcass or the same weight of raw chicken wings
* 1 onion, quartered
* 2 celery sticks, thickly sliced
* 2 carrots, thickly sliced
* 1 fresh or dried bouquet garni
* 1 tsp black peppercorns
* 1.4 litres/2½ pints cold water

Add the chicken carcass to a medium sized saucepan, add the onion, celery and carrots. Tuck in the herbs and sprinkle with the peppercorns. Pour over the water and bring just to the boil.

Partly cover and simmer gently for 1½-2 hours, skimming off any scum from time to time with a slotted spoon.

Strain through a fine sieve and leave to cool, chill until set and jellied then scoop off the thin layer of fat from the top with a spoon or using a sheet of kitchen towel. Refrigerate up to 2 days or freeze up to 3 months.

Freezer savvy

Making your own stock is not the kind of thing that many of us do on a daily basis so when you do make your own, chill it well then pack into handy sized portions in plastic freezer containers or plastic bags, seal well and label. Or freeze in sections of an ice cube tray and when frozen solid, pop the cubes out into a plastic bag. Freeze and store up to 3 months and defrost in the fridge or microwave.

Individual portions of soup make great healthy lunches too and a warming change to a sandwich and if you take a frozen block of soup to work they are pretty transportable, just make sure to double bag to avoid any leakage. Freeze the soup in plastic containers or bags. Seal well then take out in the morning and microwave to defrost and reheat. Make sure that the soup is piping hot throughout and stir well before serving.

Dressed for any occasion

Finish a bowl of soup with one of the following:

Ovenbaked croutons — Rather than frying cubes of bread in butter, spray cubes of bread with a little olive oil from a new water spray. Sprinkle with chopped rosemary, chopped garlic, a few fennel seeds or crushed dried red chillies. Bake at 180°C, 350°F, Gas Mark 4 for 10-15 minutes, turning once or twice until crispy. For pitta bread croutons, dice stale pitta breads, spray with olive oil and sprinkle with crushed cumin and coriander seeds and bake as above.

Yogurt swirls — Rather than full fat cream swirls, top a purèed soup with a spoonful of natural low fat yogurt, drizzle with a little mango chutney or a little Thai sweet chilli sauce and run the handle of a teaspoon through the mixture for a ripple effect.

Soy glazed toasted seeds and nuts — Fry a mix of sesame seeds, pumpkin seeds and cashew nuts in a little sunflower oil then drizzle over a little reduced salt soy sauce and take off the heat. When cold sprinkle over the top of the soup. Store any leftovers in a screw topped jar in the fridge.

Flavoured soft cheese — Add richness with a spoonful of reduced fat soft cheese - flavour with a little grated lemon rind, chopped chives or chopped garlic and add a small spoonful to the centre of the bowl of soup.

Herb oil — Mix 15g/½ oz finely chopped mixed herbs or finely chopped mint and ¼ teaspoon of caster sugar into 3 tablespoons of olive oil. Drizzle over the soup just before serving.

Energy

Carrot & almond soup

Per serving: 536 cals 42.6g fat 11g sat fat 20.6g protein 23.3g carbs 6.5g fibre

Adding blanched almonds to this soup along with the carrots gives it a unique and substantial consistency and makes it a filling meal.

Serves 4

* 2 tbsp olive oil
* 1 yellow onion, diced
* 2 garlic cloves, very finely chopped
* 450 g/1 lb carrots, sliced
* 1 tsp salt
* 1½ tsp ground cumin
* ½ tsp ground coriander
* ½ tsp pepper
* ½ tsp cayenne pepper
* 1 tsp sweet paprika
* ¼ tsp ground ginger
* 1.5 litres/2½ pints chicken stock
* 35 g/1¼ oz blanched almonds
* 225 g/8 oz Spanish chorizo, diced
* 55 g/2 oz flaked almonds
* juice of 1 lemon
* 15 g/½ oz fresh coriander leaves, roughly chopped

Time to get started

Put the oil into a large saucepan and heat over a medium-high heat. Add the onion and garlic and cook for 5 minutes, stirring frequently, until the onion is soft. Add the carrots, salt, cumin, ground coriander, pepper, cayenne pepper, paprika and ginger and cook, stirring, for a further minute. Add the stock and blanched almonds and bring to the boil. Reduce the heat to low and simmer, uncovered, for about 20 minutes, until the carrots are very soft.

Meanwhile, heat a heavy frying pan over a medium-high heat. Add the chorizo and cook for 6-8 minutes, stirring frequently, until the fat begins to render and the meat begins to brown. Add the flaked almonds and continue to cook, stirring frequently, until the meat is brown and the almonds are golden and crisp. Transfer to a plate lined with kitchen paper to drain.

Purée the soup with a hand-held blender until smooth. Bring to a simmer over a medium heat, then stir in the lemon juice and fresh coriander.

Ladle the soup into warmed bowls, garnish with the crispy chorizo and flaked almonds and serve immediately.

Jerusalem artichoke soup

Per serving: 285 cals 17g fat 7.4g sat fat 5.3g protein 30.9g carbs 2.7g fibre

The flavour of the knobbly artichoke is nutty. Its texture also produces a very creamy soup, without the addition of cream.

Serves 6

* 55 g/2 oz butter
* 2 onions, chopped
* 675 g/1 lb 8 oz Jerusalem artichokes, sliced and dropped into water to prevent discoloration
* 850 ml/1½ pints vegetable stock
* 300 ml/10 fl oz milk
* salt and pepper (optional)

Croûtons

* 4 tbsp vegetable oil
* 2 slices of day-old white bread, crusts removed, cut into 1-cm/½-inch cubes

How to make it

To make the croûtons, heat the oil in a frying pan over a medium heat. Add the croûtons in a single layer and fry, tossing occasionally, until golden brown and crisp.

Remove the pan from the heat and transfer the croûtons to kitchen paper to drain.

Melt the butter in a large saucepan over a medium heat. Add the onions and cook until soft.

Add the drained artichokes and mix well with the butter. Cover the pan and cook slowly over a low heat for about 10 minutes.

Pour in the stock, bring to the boil, then reduce the heat and simmer, covered, for 20 minutes.

Remove from the heat and leave to cool slightly. Blend in the saucepan using a hand-held blender. Stir in the milk, season to taste with salt and pepper, if using, then return the soup to the heat and heat until hot.

Ladle the soup into warmed bowls, sprinkle over the croûtons and serve immediately.

Amazing Artichokes

These root vegetables are one of our richest sources of the fibre inulin, which supports good digestive health, crucial in the quest to stay young.

Split pea & ham soup

Per serving: 385 cals   5.1g fat   1.3g sat fat   29g protein   58.3g carbs   22.3g fibre

This heartwarming soup benefits from the long, slow cooking process used in this recipe.

Serves 6

* 500 g/1 lb 2 oz split green peas
* 1 tbsp olive oil
* 1 large onion, finely chopped
* 1 large carrot, finely chopped
* 1 celery stick, finely chopped
* 1 litre/1¾ pints chicken stock or vegetable stock
* 1 litre/1¾ pints water
* 225 g/8 oz lean smoked ham, finely diced
* ¼ tsp dried thyme
* ¼ tsp dried marjoram
* 1 bay leaf
* salt and pepper (optional)

Slow and steady

Rinse the peas under cold running water. Put them in a saucepan and cover generously with water. Bring to the boil and boil for 3 minutes, skimming off the foam from the surface. Drain the peas.

Heat the oil in a large saucepan over a medium heat. Add the onion and cook for 3–4 minutes, stirring occasionally, until just softened. Add the carrot and celery and continue cooking for 2 minutes.

Add the peas, pour over the stock and water and stir to combine.

Bring just to the boil and stir the ham into the soup. Add the thyme, marjoram and bay leaf. Reduce the heat, cover and cook gently for 1–1½ hours, until the ingredients are very soft. Remove and discard the bay leaf.

Taste and add salt and pepper, if using. Ladle into warmed bowls and serve immediately.

Know your onions

The onion is a top health food, containing sulphur compounds that are natural antibiotics offering protection from cancers and heart disease. The vegetable also has anti-inflammatory and antibacterial action and can help minimise the nasal congestion of a cold.

Vegetable soup with pistou sauce

Per serving: 265 cals   15.7g fat   2.8g sat fat   9.6g protein   21.7g carbs   8g fibre

Packed with all things good, this vegetarian soup offers fresh produce in abundance. It's a pleasing filler as well, leaving you delightfully satisfied after devouring a bowl.

Serves 6

* 500 g/1 lb 2 oz tomatoes, peeled, deseeded and diced
* 85 g/3 oz French beans, cut into bite-sized pieces
* 1 fennel bulb, quartered and sliced
* 1 carrot, diced
* 1 courgette, diced
* 1 bouquet garni of fresh flat-leaf parsley, thyme sprigs and a bay leaf
* pinch of sugar
* 2 tbsp tomato purée
* 85 g/3 oz shelled broad beans or 85 g/3 oz shelled peas
* 400 g/14 oz canned haricot beans, drained and rinsed
* 2 tbsp small dried soup pasta, such as ditalini, or broken spaghetti pieces
* salt and pepper (optional)

Pistou sauce

* 3 garlic cloves, roughly chopped
* 55 g/2 oz basil leaves
* 30 g/1 oz Parmesan cheese, grated, plus 10 g/¼ oz extra, to serve
* pinch of coarse sea salt
* 6 tbsp extra virgin olive oil

How to make it

Put the tomatoes, French beans, fennel, carrot, courgette, bouquet garni, sugar and tomato purée into a large, heavy-based saucepan. Pour in enough water to cover the vegetables by 7.5 cm/3 inches and season generously with salt and pepper, if using. Cover the pan and bring to the boil, then stir well, reduce the heat to very low and simmer for 40–45 minutes, or until the vegetables are very tender.

Meanwhile, to make the pistou sauce, crush the garlic in a large mortar. Add the basil, cheese and salt and use the pestle to grind together until blended. Stir in the oil, tablespoon by tablespoon, then transfer to a bowl and set aside.

Uncover the soup and increase the heat to a slow boil. Add the broad beans and canned beans and boil for 5–10 minutes, or until the broad beans are tender. Add the pasta and boil for 3–5 minutes, or until the pasta is tender but still firm to the bite. The soup should be very chunky, but stir in extra water with the beans if too much liquid has evaporated.

Remove the bouquet garni and stir in the pistou sauce. Ladle into warmed bowls and serve immediately with the extra cheese for adding at the table.

Wholegrains

Choose from wholegrains such as wheatberries, farro, spelt, einkorn or emmer wheat grains, whole oat grains, sometimes called oat groats (don't confuse with porridge oats) and wholegrain rice. High in fibre they help maintain a healthy digestive tract and aid good heart health as the high amounts of soluble fibre help to reduce cholesterol. Rich in complex carbohydrates, they are digested slowly to provide a slow release form of energy without the highs and lows of refined carbs and sugar.

Quick chicken laksa

Per serving: 262 cals 9g fat 6.1g sat fat 16.5g protein 30.5g carbs 3g fibre

This mildly spiced noodle broth is a creamy, tasty delight. Don't feel you have to stick to the vegetables listed below, any of your favourites can be successfully added.

Serves 8

* 850 ml/1½ pints canned low fat coconut milk
* 200 ml/7 fl oz chicken stock
* 2-3 tbsp laksa paste
* 3 skinless, boneless chicken breasts, about 175 g/6 oz each, sliced into strips
* 250 g/9 oz cherry tomatoes, halved
* 250 g/9 oz mangetout, halved diagonally
* 200 g/7 oz dried rice noodles
* 2 tbsp fresh coriander, roughly chopped

Create your soup

Pour the coconut milk and stock into a saucepan and stir in the laksa paste. Add the chicken strips and simmer for 10-15 minutes over a gentle heat, or until the chicken is cooked through.

Stir in the tomatoes, mangetout and noodles. Simmer for an additional 2-3 minutes. Ladle into warmed bowls, garnish with the coriander and serve immediately.

Tasty Tomatoes

Tomatoes are a major source of dietary lycopene, a carotene antioxidant that fights heart disease and may help to prevent prostate cancer. Tomatoes also contain the antioxidants vitamin C, quercetin and lutein.

Mediterranean fish soup with aïoli

Per serving: 941 cals 73.5g fat 12g sat fat 65.8g protein 4.8g carbs trace fibre

Capture the taste of the Mediterranean with this deliciously chunky soup packed with a multitude of fishy goodness.

Serves 4

* 2 kg/4 lb 8 oz mixed white fish, such as gurnard, red mullet, snapper, grouper and haddock, filleted, with bones, heads and trimmings reserved
* 2 tbsp white wine vinegar
* 2 tbsp lemon juice
* 1.7 litres/3 pints vegetable stock
* 2 tsp herbes de Provence
* 2 bay leaves
* 4 egg yolks
* salt (optional)
* croûtes, to serve (optional)

Aïoli

* 4 garlic cloves
* pinch of salt
* 2 egg yolks
* 125 ml/4 fl oz extra virgin olive oil
* 125 ml/4 fl oz sunflower or safflower oil
* 1–2 tbsp lemon juice

Time to get started

Cut out and discard the gills of any reserved fish heads. Cut the fish fillets into chunks and set aside. Put the fish bones, heads and trimmings into a saucepan, pour in the vinegar, half the lemon juice and the stock, add the herbes de Provence and bay leaves and bring to the boil. Season to taste with salt, if using, reduce the heat and simmer for 30 minutes.

Meanwhile, make the aïoli. Place the garlic and salt into a mortar and pound to a paste with a pestle. Transfer to a bowl, add the egg yolks and whisk briefly with an electric mixer until creamy. Mix together the oils in a jug and, whisking constantly, gradually add them to the egg mixture. When about half the oil has been incorporated, add the remainder in a thin, steady stream, whisking constantly. Stir in lemon juice to thin to the desired consistency. Transfer the aïoli to a sauce boat, cover and set aside.

Strain the cooking liquid from the saucepan into a bowl, measure and make up to 1.7 litres/3 pints with water, if necessary. Return to the saucepan, discarding the fish heads, bones and trimmings and the bay leaves.

Beat the egg yolks with the remaining lemon juice in a bowl and stir it into the pan. Add the chunks of fish, stir gently to mix and cook over a low heat for 7–8 minutes, until the fish is just cooked through. Do not allow the soup to boil. Remove from the heat and ladle into warmed bowls. Serve immediately with the aïoli and croûtes, if wished.

Roasted butternut squash soup with orange & fennel

Per serving: 499 cals 38.7g fat 18.8g sat fat 5.3g protein 39g carbs 6.6g fibre

Squash makes for a popular soup loved by many. Try this fantastically different variation with orange and fennel for a real tasty treat.

Serves 4

* 2 dried chipotle chillies
* 1 large butternut squash, peeled, cut in half, deseeded, and cut into 2.5-cm/1-inch cubes
* 2 tbsp extra virgin olive oil, plus 1 tbsp extra for brushing
* 2 tbsp unsalted butter
* 1 small fennel bulb, trimmed and chopped, fronds reserved for garnish
* 2 shallots, chopped
* 2 garlic cloves, chopped
* 1 tsp finely grated orange zest
* 2 tsp ground cumin
* 175 ml/6 fl oz orange juice
* 225 ml/8 fl oz water
* 225 ml/8 fl oz double cream
* 1 tbsp fresh lemon juice, or to taste
* salt (optional)

How to make it

Preheat the oven to 190°C/ 375°F/Gas Mark 5 and oil a baking pan. Preheat a small, heavy frying pan (preferably cast iron) over medium heat. Place the chillies on the skillet, pressing down on them with a spatula for about 20 seconds to lightly toast, then turn over and toast on the other side for about 20 seconds. Remove the chillies from the skillet and place them in a bowl. Pour in hot water to cover and soak for about 30 minutes, or until fully hydrated, stirring occasionally or placing a plate on top of the chillies to keep them submerged. Drain the chillies and discard the soaking liquid. Remove the stems and seeds from the chillies and chop very finely.

Place the squash in a large bowl, add the oil, and toss to coat. Sprinkle with salt, if using, and toss. Place the squash in the baking pan in one layer and bake for about 45 minutes, until browned and tender when pierced with a fork, turning the pieces occasionally. Return the squash to the bowl.

Warm the butter in a large saucepan over medium–low heat. Add the fennel, shallots, garlic, orange zest and chillies. Cover the pan and cook for 15 minutes, or until the vegetables are softened but not browned. Add the cumin and stir for 1 minute. Increase the heat, add the squash, orange juice, and water and bring to a simmer. Partially cover the pan and simmer for 15 minutes to combine the flavours. Add the cream and simmer for 5 minutes. Season to taste with salt, if using.

Transfer the soup, in batches, to a blender and blend until smooth, adding water if needed to reach desired consistency. Return the soup to the pan and add the lemon juice and salt to taste, if needed. Gently rewarm. Ladle into warmed bowls, garnish with the fennel fronds, and serve immediately.

Energizing beef, beetroot & apple soup

Per serving: 299 cals   10.5g fat   3.9g sat fat   20.8g protein   33.6g carbs   7.9g fibre

Beetroot juice has been a favourite performance booster for athletes for a while. Combined with protein-boosting beef and cholesterol-lowering apples, this light fresh soup will energize and reinvigorate you for the afternoon ahead.

Serves 4

* 1 tbsp olive oil
* 250 g/9 oz lean braising steak, trimmed of all fat, cut into small dice
* 1 onion, finely chopped
* 600 g/1lb 5 oz uncooked beetroot, coarsely grated
* 115 g/4 oz carrots, coarsely grated
* 2 dessert apples, 1 cored and coarsely grated
* 1 tsp mild paprika
* 1 tsp caraway seeds
* 1 tsp fennel seeds
* 1 litre/1¾ pints beef stock
* 1 tbsp red wine vinegar
* 150 g/5½ oz fat-free natural Greek-style yogurt
* 2 tbsp chopped fresh dill
* salt and pepper (optional)

Meal in a bowl

Heat the oil in a large saucepan, add the beef and fry over a medium heat, stirring, for 5 minutes until brown all over. Add the onion and cook for 5 minutes, stirring, until lightly coloured.

Add the beetroot, carrot and grated apple. Sprinkle over the paprika, caraway seeds and fennel seeds, then pour in the stock. Add the vinegar and bring to the boil, stirring. Cover and simmer, stirring occasionally, for 45 minutes until the beef is tender.

When the soup is ready, add salt and pepper to taste, if using. Core the remaining apple and cut into small dice. Ladle the soup into warmed bowls, then top with the yogurt, diced apple and dill and serve immediately.

Beef it up!

Lean beef is a fine source of top quality protein. Lean beef – especially grass-fed – is lower in total fat and saturates than many other foods and other meats and it is quite safe to eat 1-2 small portions a week.

Power-boosting chipotle chilli & black bean soup

Per serving: 316 cals   10.3g fat   3.2g sat fat   20.8g protein   34g carbs   11g fibre

This energy-packed high performance soup, packed with slow-release healthy carbs, mixed vegetables rich in cancer-fighting antioxidants and protein-rich lean diced beef will provide a sustaining lunch.

Serves 4

* 1 dried chipotle chilli
* 3 tbsp boiling water
* 1 tbsp olive oil
* 250 g/9 oz lean braising steak, trimmed of all fat, cut into small dice
* 1 onion, finely chopped
* 1 garlic clove, finely chopped
* 350 g/12 oz sweet potatoes, diced
* 450 g/1 lb tomatoes, peeled and diced
* 1 tsp cumin seeds, roughly crushed
* ½ tsp ground cinnamon
* 600 ml/1 pint beef stock
* 230 g/8¼ oz canned black beans in water, drained weight
* 1 tbsp tomato purée
* 2 tsp dark muscovado sugar
* salt and pepper (optional)

Create your soup

Put the chilli into a small bowl, cover with the boiling water and set aside for 5 minutes to soak.

Heat the oil in a large saucepan, add the meat and fry over a medium heat, stirring, for 5 minutes until brown all over. Add the onion and cook for 5 minutes, stirring, until lightly coloured.

Stir the garlic into the onion, then add the sweet potatoes and tomatoes. Sprinkle in the cumin seeds and cinnamon, then pour in the stock. Add the beans, tomato purée and sugar.

Lift the chilli out of the water and finely chop, then add the chilli (with the seeds) to the pan together with the soaking water and bring to the boil, stirring. Cover and simmer for 45 minutes, stirring occasionally, until the meat is tender. Add salt and pepper to taste, if using. Ladle into warmed bowls and serve immediately.

Energizing beef,
beetroot & apple soup
page 30

Power-boosting
chipotle chilli & black
bean soup
page 31

Layered pork & spiced sauerkraut soup

The probiotics found in fermented vegetables such as sauerkraut are thought to help boost the good bacteria in your gut, which can help maintain your immune system, keep your digestive tract healthy and contribute to a feeling of well-being.

Serves 4

* 1 tbsp olive oil
* 350 g/12 oz pork fillet, thinly sliced
* 1 onion, chopped
* 2 garlic cloves, finely chopped
* 850 ml/1½ pints chicken stock
* 1 tsp fennel seeds
* 1 tsp English mustard
* 175 g/6 oz Brussels sprouts, thinly sliced
* 1 tsp caraway seeds
* 115 g/4 oz carrots, coarsely grated
* 1 dessert apple, cored and coarsely grated
* 175 g/6 oz sauerkraut, drained
* 70 g/2½ oz gherkins, drained and diced
* 2 tbsp chopped fresh dill
* salt and pepper (optional)

How to make it

Heat the oil in a saucepan, add the pork and fry, stirring, for 5 minutes until brown. Add the onion and fry for 5 minutes until lightly coloured.

Mix in the garlic and stock, then add the fennel seeds and mustard. Bring to the boil, then cover and simmer for 30 minutes.

When the pork is almost cooked, mix the sprouts with the caraway seeds and steam for 5 minutes until just tender.

Divide half the pork mixture between four large heatproof tumblers, arranging it on the base. Mix the carrot and apple and spoon into the glasses, then top with the steamed sprouts, followed by the remaining pork. Mix the sauerkraut with the gherkins and the chopped dill, then spoon the mixture into the glasses.

Season the hot broth with salt and pepper to taste, if using, then pour it into the tumblers until all the vegetables are just covered. Serve immediately.

Per serving: 215 cals   6.8g fat   1.7g sat fat   21.5g protein   18.9g carbs   5.4g fibre

Squash, sweet potato & garlic soup

Per serving: 207 cals 10.5g fat 4.6g sat fat 3g protein 28.2g carbs 4g fibre

Squashes can be stuffed and baked or skinned and roasted as an alternative to white potatoes. Here, they make a perfectly delicious winter warmer soup.

Serves 6

* 1 acorn or butternut squash
* 1 sweet potato, about 350 g/12 oz
* 4 shallots
* 2 tbsp olive oil
* 5–6 garlic cloves, unpeeled
* 850 ml/1½ pints chicken stock
* 100 ml/3½ fl oz crème fraîche
* pepper (optional)
* 3 tbsp snipped fresh chives, to garnish

Blend it

Preheat the oven to 190°C/375°F/Gas Mark 5. Cut the squash, sweet potato and shallots in half lengthways, through to the stem end. Scoop the seeds out of the squash. Brush the cut sides with the oil.

Place the vegetables, cut-side down, in a shallow roasting tin and add the garlic. Roast in the preheated oven for about 40 minutes until tender and light brown. Cool.

When cool, scoop the flesh from the sweet potato and squash halves and place in a saucepan with the shallots. Peel the garlic and add the soft insides to the other vegetables.

Add the stock. Bring just to the boil, reduce the heat and simmer, partially covered, for about 30 minutes, stirring occasionally, until the vegetables are very tender.

Leave the soup to cool slightly, then transfer to a food processor and process until smooth, working in batches, if necessary. (If using a food processor, strain off the cooking liquid and set aside. Process the soup solids with enough cooking liquid to moisten them, then combine with the remaining liquid.)

Return the soup to the rinsed-out saucepan. Season to taste with pepper, if using, then simmer for 5–10 minutes, until completely heated through. Ladle into warmed bowls and swirl over the crème fraîche. Garnish with extra pepper and snipped chives and serve immediately.

Spicy chicken noodle soup

A refreshing, zingy and super-tasty soup that is easy to make but still offers a real wow-factor.

Serves 2

* 2-cm/¾-inch piece fresh ginger
* 1 red chilli
* 1 carrot
* 200 g/7 oz pak choi
* 1 cooked chicken breast
* 300 ml/10 fl oz chicken stock
* 18 g/¾ oz miso paste
* 150 g/5½ oz straight-to-wok egg thread noodles
* dark soy sauce, to taste (optional)
* 4 spring onions

Meal in a bowl

Peel the ginger, deseed and finely dice the chilli and cut the carrot into thin strips. Roughly chop the pak choi and shred the chicken. Put the stock into a large saucepan with 250 ml/9 fl oz boiling water and bring to the boil over a medium–high heat. Add the miso paste and simmer for 1–2 minutes.

Add the chilli, carrot, pak choi, noodles and chicken and grate in the ginger. Simmer for a further 4–5 minutes.

Add soy sauce to taste, if using. Trim and finely chop the spring onions and scatter them in the base of two warmed bowls. Pour the soup over and serve immediately.

Feeling hot, hot, hot!

Chillies contain capsaicin, which can relieve pain and inflammation associated with arthritis. They're also rich in vitamin C and carotenes to help boost the immune system.

Vegetable noodle broth

Per serving: 554 cals   14.6g fat   3.5g sat fat   19.1g protein   90.5g carbs   8.9g fibre

This fantastically light Oriental broth is packed with healthy vegetables and bursting with flavourful spices.

Serves 4

* 400 g/14 oz dried thick egg noodles
* 2 tbsp vegetable or groundnut oil
* 1 onion, finely chopped
* 1 tsp ground cumin
* ½ tsp ground turmeric
* 2 garlic cloves, crushed
* 2 tsp grated fresh ginger
* 1 tsp salt
* 2 fresh green chillies, finely chopped
* 100 g/3½ oz mangetout, thinly sliced lengthways
* 2 large carrots, cut into matchsticks
* 1 red pepper, deseeded and thinly sliced
* 2 tomatoes, finely chopped
* 2 tbsp dark soy sauce
* 1 litre/1¾ pints vegetable stock
* 1 tsp pepper
* 200 g/7 oz baby spinach leaves
* 6 tbsp finely chopped fresh coriander
* 1 tsp toasted sesame oil

Time to get started

Cook the noodles according to the packet instructions. Drain, rinse with cold water and set aside.

Meanwhile, heat the vegetable oil in a large saucepan over a medium heat, add the onion and stir-fry for 8–10 minutes, or until lightly browned.

Add the cumin, turmeric, garlic, ginger, salt and chillies to the pan and stir-fry for 1–2 minutes. Add the mangetout, carrots and red pepper and stir-fry for a further 1–2 minutes.

Add the tomatoes, soy sauce, stock and pepper. Bring to the boil, then reduce the heat and simmer for 10–12 minutes, until the vegetables are tender.

Add the reserved noodles and the spinach and bring back to the boil. Stir until the spinach wilts, then remove from the heat and stir in the chopped coriander and sesame oil. Ladle into warmed bowls and serve immediately.

Spiced lamb & chickpea broth

Per serving: 317 cals 11.8g fat 3.9g sat fat 19.4g protein 35g carbs 8g fibre

This Moroccan-inspired broth-based soup is packed with meaty goodness, chickpeas and sweet potatoes, the good guy carbs full of slow-release energy. It is finished with a fresh mint topping.

Serves 4

* 1 tbsp olive oil
* 750 g/1lb 10 oz neck of lamb on the bone
* 2 onions, roughly chopped
* 2 garlic cloves, sliced
* 7.5-cm/3-inch piece cinnamon stick, halved
* 4 cloves
* 30 g/1 oz fresh ginger, sliced
* 1 tsp cumin seeds, roughly crushed
* ¼ tsp black peppercorns, roughly crushed
* 1.4 litres/2½ pints lamb stock
* 400 g/14 oz canned chickpeas in water, drained
* 200 g/7 oz carrots, diced
* 300 g/10½ oz sweet potatoes, diced
* ½ tsp hot smoked paprika
* 2 tbsp chopped fresh mint
* salt (optional)

How to make it

Heat the oil in a large saucepan, then add the lamb and brown over a medium heat on one side for 5 minutes. Turn the pieces over, add the onions and fry, stirring the onions and turning the lamb as needed, for 10 minutes until brown.

Add the garlic, cinnamon, cloves, ginger, cumin seeds and peppercorns, then pour in the stock. Bring to the boil, stirring, then cover and simmer for 1½ hours until the meat is very tender and almost falling off the bones.

Lift the meat out of the pan with a slotted spoon and transfer to a plate. Strain the soup into a separate saucepan. Add the chickpeas, carrots, sweet potatoes and paprika and bring to the boil, stirring. Cover and simmer for 30 minutes until the vegetables are tender.

Meanwhile, cut any fat from the lamb, pull the meat from the bones and cut into small pieces. You should have about 225 g/8 oz. Return the meat to the soup for the last 10 minutes of cooking. Taste the soup and add a little salt, if using. Ladle into warmed bowls, sprinkle with the chopped mint and serve immediately

Clams in bacon, leek & cream broth

Per serving: 369 cals 21.8g fat 10.9g sat fat 18.9g protein 10.3g carbs 1.1g fibre

The bacon really complements the clams in this recipe, adding a little saltiness. When buying your bacon, try to find a brand that has no sugar in the cure for a healthier low-sugar version.

Serves 4

* 1.5 kg/3 lb 5 oz live clams, scrubbed
* 1 tsp butter
* 12 streaky bacon rashers, roughly chopped
* 200 g/7 oz leeks, sliced
* 1 garlic clove, finely chopped
* 100 ml/3½ fl oz brandy
* 300 ml/10 fl oz cold water
* 100 ml/3½ fl oz single cream
* 25 g/1 oz fresh flat-leaf parsley, finely chopped

To make this soup

Discard any clams with broken shells or any that refuse to close when tapped.

Melt the butter in a deep, heavy-based saucepan over a medium heat. Add the bacon and fry, stirring, for 4–5 minutes, or until crisp and golden. Using a slotted spoon, transfer to a plate lined with kitchen paper.

Put the leeks and garlic in the pan and cook, stirring regularly, for 5 minutes, or until softened but not browned.

Pour in the brandy and leave it to bubble for a minute to burn off the alcohol (brandy in a hot pan can easily flame, so take care). Add the water and stir well. Turn up the heat to medium–high and, when the water starts to boil, toss in the clams. Put on the lid and steam for 5 minutes, or until the clams have opened.

Take the pan off the heat. Discard any clams that remain closed. Stir in the bacon and cream. Sprinkle with the parsley and serve in warmed bowls, with a large empty bowl to collect the shells.

Don't clam up!

All edible clams are highly nutritious, being low in fat and high in a wide range of minerals and B vitamins. Clams have a particularly high iron content and just 100 g/3½ oz of shelled clams provide a whole day's intake.

Chickpea, saffron & lemon chermoula soup

Per serving: 228 cals 9.8g fat 2g sat fat 5.8g protein 32.2g carbs 6.7g fibre

This Moroccan-inspired soup is both healthy and hearty with the chermoula giving an unexpected yet delicious twist.

Serves 4

* 2 tbsp olive oil
* 1 leek, sliced
* 1 onion, chopped
* 1 celery stick, sliced
* 1 carrot, sliced
* 2 garlic cloves, crushed
* 1 tbsp coriander seeds
* 115 g/4 oz canned tomatoes
* 140 g/5 oz canned chickpeas, drained and rinsed
* 1 litre/1¾ pints vegetable stock
* 1 potato, diced
* 2 bay leaves
* pinch of saffron strands
* 2 lemons, halved, cut sides charred for 2–5 minutes in a hot non-stick frying pan

Chermoula

* 2 garlic cloves, finely sliced
* ½ red chilli, finely chopped
* 1 tsp paprika
* 1 tsp ground cumin
* 1 tsp lemon juice
* 2 tsp white wine vinegar
* 4 tbsp finely chopped fresh flat-leaf parsley
* 4 tbsp finely chopped fresh coriander leaves

Blend it

Heat the oil in a large saucepan and sauté the leek, onion, celery, carrot and garlic, stirring constantly, for 5 minutes, or until softened but not coloured. Add the coriander seeds and cook for a further 2 minutes.

Add the tomatoes, chickpeas, stock, potato, bay leaves and saffron. Stir well and bring to the boil. Reduce the heat, cover and simmer for 20 minutes, or until the vegetables are tender.

To make the chermoula, pound the garlic and chilli with the spices, lemon juice and vinegar to a smooth paste in a mortar with a pestle. Transfer to a saucepan, add the herbs and gently warm for 5 minutes to infuse the flavours. Do not boil.

Remove and discard the bay leaves, then blend the soup using a food processor or blender. Pass through a medium sieve into warmed soup bowls. Top with the chermoula and serve with the charred lemons for squeezing over.

Seven seas soup

Per serving: 295 cals 8.5g fat 2.3g sat fat 26.2g protein 31g carbs 5.4g fibre

High in protein, vitamins and minerals, fish is low in calories. Mixed with Mediterranean vegetables and brown rice, this light and energizing soup will zap your taste buds and refuel your system without you feeling as though you need a siesta.

Serves 4

* 1 tbsp olive oil
* 1 onion, finely chopped
* 2 garlic cloves, finely chopped
* 1 small fennel bulb, green fronds reserved, bulb finely chopped
* 1 red pepper, halved, deseeded and diced
* 500 g/1 lb 2 oz tomatoes, peeled and diced
* 1.2 litres/2 pints vegetable stock
* 55 g/2 oz short-grain brown rice
* ½ tsp dried oregano
* ¼ tsp crushed dried red chillies
* 1 tbsp tomato purée
* 40 g/1½ oz canned dressed brown crabmeat
* 150 g/5½ oz prepared squid, sliced, thawed if frozen
* 225 g/8 oz raw prawns, peeled and deveined and thawed if frozen
* 225 g/8 oz cooked, shelled mussels, thawed if frozen
* 2 tbsp chopped fresh parsley
* grated rind of 1 lemon
* salt and pepper (optional)

Time to get started

Heat the oil in a large saucepan, add the onion and fry over a medium heat, stirring, for 5 minutes until soft and just beginning to colour. Stir in the garlic, fennel, red pepper and tomatoes and cook for 3 minutes.

Pour in the stock, then add the rice, oregano, chillies and tomato purée. Bring to the boil, stirring, then cover and simmer for 30 minutes until the rice is tender.

Stir the crabmeat into the soup, then add the squid, prawns and mussels and cook for 5 minutes until all the prawns are bright pink. Add salt and pepper to taste, if using.

Chop the reserved fennel fronds and mix with the parsley and lemon rind. Ladle the soup into warmed shallow bowls, sprinkle the herb mix on top and serve immediately.

Nourish

Chicken & leek soup

Per serving: 399 cals 14.6g fat 3g sat fat 34.4g protein 32.9g carbs 3.7g fibre

This Scottish recipe is otherwise known as cock-a-leekie and has the unusual soup ingredient of prunes, which you can easily omit if preferred.

Serves 4

* 2 tbsp olive oil
* 2 onions, roughly chopped
* 2 carrots, roughly chopped
* 5 leeks, 2 roughly chopped, 3 thinly sliced
* 1 chicken, weighing 1.3 kg/3 lb
* 2 bay leaves
* 6 prunes, sliced
* salt and pepper (optional)
* 4 fresh parsley sprigs, to garnish

Time to get started

Heat the oil in a large saucepan. Add the onions, carrots and the 2 roughly chopped leeks and sauté over a medium heat for 3–4 minutes, until just golden brown.

Wipe the chicken inside and out and remove as much skin and fat as you can – the breast skin will come away easily with your fingers and the leg skin can be removed carefully with a small sharp knife slid between the flesh and skin. Fat clings inside the cavity and on the underside of the bird.

Place the chicken in the saucepan with the cooked vegetables and add the bay leaves. Pour in enough cold water to just cover and season well with salt and pepper, if using. Bring to the boil, reduce the heat, then cover and simmer for 1–1½ hours, skimming off any foam that rises to the surface with a slotted spoon.

Remove the chicken from the stock, remove and discard any remaining bits of skin, then remove all the meat. Cut the meat into neat pieces. Strain the stock through a colander, discarding the vegetables and bay leaves, and return to the rinsed-out saucepan. Expect to have 1.2–1.4 litres/2–2½ pints of stock. If you have time, it is a good idea to allow the stock to cool so that the fat may be removed. If not, blot the fat off the surface with pieces of kitchen paper.

Heat the stock to simmering point. Add the sliced leeks and prunes and heat for about 1 minute.

Return the chicken to the pan and heat through. Ladle the soup into warmed bowls and serve immediately, garnished with parsley sprigs.

Quinoa, chestnut & mushroom soup

Per serving: 249 cals   10.4g fat   1.7g sat fat   9g protein   31.2g carbs   5.3g fibre

Quick and easy to cook, this earthy autumnal soup is perfect on a cold day. Quinoa is the least allergenic of all the grains and one of the few grains that contains all 9 essential amino acids, the building blocks that make up protein.

Serves 4

* 20 g/¾ oz dried porcini mushrooms
* 225 ml/8 fl oz boiling water
* 2 tbsp olive oil
* 1 onion, finely chopped
* 400 g/14 oz closed-cup chestnut mushrooms, sliced
* 1 garlic clove, finely chopped
* 450 ml/16 fl oz vegetable stock
* 3 fresh thyme sprigs
* 85 g/3 oz red quinoa
* 450 ml/16 fl oz unsweetened almond milk
* 100 g/3½ oz vacuum-packed ready peeled chestnuts
* 3 tbsp chopped fresh parsley
* salt and pepper (optional)

To make this soup

Put the dried mushrooms into a bowl, pour over the boiling water and leave to soak for 15 minutes.

Meanwhile, heat 1 tablespoon of the oil in a saucepan, add the onion and cook, stirring, for 5 minutes until soft and just beginning to colour. Add the remaining oil, sliced chestnut mushrooms and garlic and fry, stirring, for 3–4 minutes until just beginning to turn golden.

Pour in the stock, add the thyme and quinoa and bring to the boil. Add the soaked mushrooms and the soaking liquid, then cover and simmer for 15 minutes.

Remove and discard the thyme, stir in the almond milk and crumble in the chestnuts. Bring to the boil, then add salt and pepper to taste, if using. Ladle into warmed bowls, sprinkle with the chopped parsley and serve immediately.

Keen on quinoa

Quinoa provides the essential amino acids needed to make proteins, which are crucial for reproduction. It also has a rich mineral and B-vitamin content.

Kale & summer garden herb soup

Per serving: 162 cals 7g fat 1.2g sat fat 3.5g protein 24.3g carbs 6g fibre

This bright green soup not only looks good but does you good too. Kale can sometimes taste a little strong but it is balanced here with fresh-tasting herbs and the natural sweetness of parsnip.

Serves 4

* 1 tbsp olive oil
* 1 onion, chopped
* 200 g/7 oz parsnips, diced
* 4 celery sticks, sliced
* 600 ml/1 pint vegetable stock
* 115 g/4 oz kale, shredded
* 25 g/1 oz mixed fresh garden herbs, leaves only
* 2 tbsp ground linseeds
* 300 ml/10 fl oz unsweetened rice milk
* salt and pepper (optional)

How to make it

Heat the oil in a saucepan, add the onion and fry over a medium heat, stirring, for 5 minutes until soft. Add the parsnips and celery, then pour in the stock. Bring to the boil, stirring, then cover and simmer for 20 minutes, or until the parsnips are tender.

Stir in the kale, herbs and ground linseeds, then cover and cook for 3–4 minutes until the kale has just wilted but is still bright green.

Purée the soup in a blender or food processor. Return to the pan and stir in the rice milk. Bring to the boil, stirring, then season with salt and pepper to taste, if using. Ladle into warmed bowls or mugs and serve immediately.

Kale & summer
garden herb soup
page 53

Quinoa, chestnut &
mushroom soup
page 52

Layered avocado & strawberry soup

Chilled soups are wonderfully refreshing and restorative. This creamy smooth avocado and watercress version is lightly cooked and puréed, then layered with raw puréed strawberries. If soups are the new juice, this version is the best of both.

Serves 4

* 1 tsp avocado oil
* 4 spring onions, sliced
* 25 g/1 oz watercress
* 250 ml/9 fl oz vegetable stock
* 1 avocado, halved, stoned and flesh scooped out
* 225 g/8 oz strawberries, hulled and halved
* juice of ½ lemon

Blend it

Heat the oil in a saucepan, add the spring onions and cook over a medium heat, stirring, for 2 minutes until soft. Add the watercress and stock and bring to the boil, stirring. Cover and simmer for 3–4 minutes until the watercress has just wilted. Leave to cool, then chill well.

Purée the chilled watercress mixture with the avocado in a blender or food processor until smooth, then pour into a jug. Rinse the blender goblet, then purée the strawberries and mix with the lemon juice. Press through a sieve into a jug.

Spoon half the avocado soup into the base of four small glass tumblers, spoon over half the strawberry mixture to give two different coloured layers, then repeat.

Serve immediately or chill for up to 45 minutes.

Per serving: 118 cals 9.1g fat 1.4g sat fat 1.9g protein 10.5g carbs 4.9g fibre

Ham hock & tomato-rice soup

Per serving: 175 cals 5.9g fat 1.8g sat fat 12.5g protein 17.5g carbs 0.5g fibre

Serves 6-8

* 1 small ham hock, about 450 g/1 lb
* 2 x 400 g/14 oz canned plum tomatoes
* 140 g/5 oz basmati rice
* ½ tsp salt
* crusty bread, to serve (optional)

Meal in a bowl

Place the ham hock in a large saucepan and add enough water to cover the ham. Bring to the boil over a medium heat, cover with a lid, reduce the heat and leave to simmer for 1 hour. Take off the heat and allow to cool slightly.

Remove the ham from the pan. Cut the meat from the bone and return it to the stock.

Bring the stock mixture to the boil, then add the canned tomatoes with their juices, rice and salt. Cover, reduce the heat and simmer for 30 minutes. Ladle into warmed bowls and serve immediately with crusty bread, if using.

Tomato time

The antioxidant lycopene is actually more active in processed tomato products such as ketchup, tomato purée and tomato juice than it is in the raw tomato.

Salmon & udon broth

Per serving: 271 cals 10.6g fat 3g sat fat 18.2g protein 26.7g carbs 3.7g fibre

A gorgeous broth that is both low in fat but also high in nutrients makes this dish a winner. The thick udon noodles turn an otherwise light meal into a feast in a bowl.

Serves 4

* 2.5-cm/1-inch piece fresh ginger
* 6 spring onions
* 2 carrots
* 1 litre/1¾ pints vegetable stock
* 30 g/1 oz miso soup paste
* 250 g/9 oz fresh salmon fillet
* 125 g/4½ oz shiitake mushrooms
* 250 g/9 oz straight-to-wok udon noodles
* 1 fresh red chilli
* dark soy sauce, to taste (optional)

How to make it

Peel and thinly slice the ginger, finely chop the spring onions and cut the carrots into thin batons. Add the ginger, spring onions and carrots to a large saucepan with the stock and miso paste and bring to the boil over a medium-high heat.

Cut the salmon into cubes and slice the mushrooms, then add to the broth and cook for 2–3 minutes, until the salmon is cooked through and flakes easily. Add the noodles and stir until heated through.

Deseed and thinly slice the chilli. Divide the soup between four warmed bowls. Add soy sauce to taste, if using, garnish with a little chilli and serve immediately.

Super salmon

Salmon is an excellent source of omega-3 fatty acids, which have several beneficial properties. Salmon is also rich in a range of vitamins and minerals, helping to protect against cancer and fight depression.

Spinach & ginger soup

Per serving: 156 cals 9.5g fat 1.7g sat fat 3.4g protein 16.5g carbs 3.5g fibre

This thick and deep green soup is much more appetizing than it looks! Paired with garlic, ginger and lemon grass, this makes for an unusual tasty treat.

Serves 4

* 2 tbsp sunflower oil
* 1 onion, chopped
* 2 garlic cloves, finely chopped
* 2 tsp finely chopped fresh ginger
* 250 g/9 oz baby spinach leaves
* 1 small lemon grass stalk, finely chopped
* 1 litre/1¾ pints chicken or vegetable stock
* 225 g/8 oz potatoes, chopped
* 1 tbsp rice wine or dry sherry
* salt and pepper (optional)
* 1 tsp sesame oil, for drizzling

Blend it

Heat the sunflower oil in a large saucepan. Add the onion, garlic and ginger, and fry gently for 3–4 minutes, until softened but not browned.

Reserve eight small spinach leaves. Add the remaining leaves and the lemon grass to the saucepan, stirring until the spinach is wilted. Add the stock and potatoes to the pan and bring to the boil. Reduce the heat, cover and simmer for about 10 minutes.

Remove the saucepan from the heat and leave to cool slightly. Transfer to a food processor or blender, in batches if necessary, and process to a purée.

Return the soup to the rinsed-out pan, stir in the rice wine and reheat gently. Taste and adjust the seasoning, adding salt and pepper if using.

Ladle into warmed bowls and top each with a drizzle of sesame oil. Garnish with the reserved spinach leaves and serve immediately.

Special spinach

Spinach contains many antioxidants that fight against stomach, skin, breast, prostate and other cancers. It is also extremely high in carotenes, which helps protect eyesight.

Chilled broad bean soup

Per serving: 190 cals 3.5g fat 1.9g sat fat 15.4g protein 20.3g carbs 10.8g fibre

Many people are shy of a chilled soup but this one is most certainly worth ringing the changes for. With zingy lemon and summer savory this recipe makes for a fresh taste sensation not to be missed.

Serves 4

* 850 ml/1½ pints vegetable stock
* 650 g/1 lb 7 oz shelled fresh young broad beans
* 3 tbsp lemon juice
* 2 tbsp chopped fresh summer savory
* salt and pepper (optional)
* 4 tbsp Greek-style yogurt, to serve
* 2 tbsp chopped fresh mint, to garnish

To make this soup

Pour the stock into a saucepan and bring to the boil. Reduce the heat to a simmer, add the broad beans and cook for about 7 minutes, until just tender.

Remove the pan from the heat and leave to cool slightly. Ladle into a food processor or blender, in batches if necessary, and process to a purée. Push the mixture through a sieve into a bowl.

Stir in the lemon juice and summer savory and season to taste with salt and pepper, if using. Leave to cool completely, then cover with clingfilm and chill in the refrigerator for at least 3 hours.

To serve, stir the soup, taste and adjust the seasoning, if neccesary. Ladle into chilled bowls, top each with a tablespoon of yogurt and garnish with mint. Serve immediately.

Broad is best

Broad beans are in season from June to mid September. Best when they're as fresh as possible, these little green gems are a great source of protein and carbohydrates, as well as vitamins A, B, B1 and B2.

Basic beef bone broth

Per serving: 90 cals 2.5g fat 1g sat fat 3.7g protein 14g carbs 1.7g fibre

Packed with minerals, this light, clear and warming broth makes a great alternative to caffeine-laden cups of tea and coffee. Don't be put off by the lengthy cooking time — once the soup is simmering you can get on with other things around the house.

Serves 4

* 2 kg/4 lb 8 oz beef bones, cut into large pieces
* 2 onions, cut into chunks
* 175 g/6 oz leeks, thickly sliced
* 225 g/8 oz carrots, thickly sliced
* 3 celery sticks, thickly sliced
* 3 tomatoes, cut into chunks
* 2 garlic cloves, halved
* 3 bay leaves
* 10-cm/4-inch piece of cinnamon stick, halved
* 85 g/3 oz fresh ginger, sliced
* 1 tbsp dark muscovado sugar
* 3 litres/5¼ pints water
* 1 tsp black peppercorns, roughly crushed
* salt (optional)

Time to get started

Preheat the oven to 220°C/425°F/Gas Mark 7. Put the beef bones into a large roasting tin and bake in the preheated oven for 30 minutes until just beginning to brown. Turn the bones over and add the onions, leeks, carrots, celery, tomatoes and garlic. Bake for about 30 minutes until the bones are a deep brown and the vegetables are tinged with colour.

Scoop the bones and vegetables from the tin with a large slotted spoon, draining off as much fat as possible, and transfer to a large saucepan.

Add the bay leaves, cinnamon, ginger and sugar to the pan, then pour over the water and mix in the peppercorns. Bring to the boil, skimming off any foam, then cover and simmer gently for 4 hours.

Pour the broth through a muslin-lined fine sieve into a large measuring jug. You should have about 1.4 litres/2½ pints. If you have a lot more, return the broth to the pan and simmer, uncovered, to reduce and concentrate the flavours. Taste and add salt, if using.

Leave to cool, then chill overnight in the refrigerator. Scoop the fat off the top with a spoon then reheat the broth, ladle into warmed mugs and serve immediately.

Beef, red onion & cranberry soup

Per serving: 308 cals 11.9g fat 4g sat fat 28g protein 24.5g carbs 3.8g fibre

Slow-cooked for maximum flavour, this warming and reviving soup has just a hint of cranberry and orange. The Puy lentils help to make a small amount of red meat go further as they take a while for the body to digest, leaving you feeling fuller for longer.

Serves 4

* 1 tbsp olive oil
* 400 g/14 oz lean braising steak, cut into small dice
* 1 red onion, chopped
* 2 celery sticks, diced
* 400 g/14 oz canned chopped tomatoes
* 1 litre/1¾ pints beef stock
* 70 g/2½ oz Puy lentils
* 2 tbsp cranberry sauce
* grated rind of ½ orange
* 150 g/5½ oz cauliflower florets, thinly sliced
* salt and pepper (optional)

Create your soup

Heat the oil in a saucepan, add the beef and fry over a medium heat, stirring, for 5 minutes until brown all over. Add the onion and fry, stirring, for 5 minutes until lightly coloured.

Stir in the celery, tomatoes and stock, then add the lentils, cranberry sauce and orange rind. Bring to the boil, stirring, then cover and simmer for 1¾ hours, stirring occasionally.

Add the cauliflower florets and simmer for 5 minutes until just tender. Add salt and pepper to taste, if using. Ladle into warmed bowls and serve immediately.

Pork adobo soup

Soup is a great way to make small quantities of meat stretch further. Slow-cooked pork with rich soy sauce, sherry and star anise make for a delicious nutrient-boosting and warming meal, at any time of the day.

Serves 4

* 1 tbsp rice bran oil
* 350 g/12 oz pork shoulder, trimmed of all fat and cut into small dice
* 1 onion, chopped
* 2 garlic cloves, finely chopped
* 1 litre/1¾ pints chicken stock
* 2 tbsp reduced-salt soy sauce
* 4 tbsp medium sherry
* 2 bay leaves
* 2 star anise
* 2 tsp tomato purée
* 1 tbsp dark muscovado sugar
* 1 tbsp rice vinegar
* 55 g/2 oz long-grain brown rice
* 115 g/4 oz carrots, cut into small strips
* 200 g/7 oz tender-stem broccoli, stems sliced, florets halved
* 115 g/4 oz beansprouts, rinsed with cold water, drained
* 3 tbsp roughly chopped fresh coriander

How to make it

Heat the oil in a saucepan, add the pork and fry, stirring, for 5 minutes until brown. Add the onion and fry for 5 minutes until just beginning to colour.

Stir in the garlic, then add the stock, soy sauce, sherry, bay leaves and star anise. Add the tomato purée, sugar, vinegar and rice and bring to the boil, stirring.

Cover and simmer for 50 minutes. When the soup is almost ready steam the carrots and broccoli for 5 minutes over a saucepan of simmering water. Remove and discard the bay leaves and star anise. Add the beansprouts and cook for 1 minute until hot.

Ladle the soup into warmed bowls, top with the steamed vegetables, sprinkle with the coriander and serve immediately.

Per serving: 299 cals 10.4g fat 3.3g sat fat 21.6g protein 28.5g carbs 4g fibre

Chorizo & kale soup

Per serving: 350 cals   19.3g fat   5.3g sat fat   11.8g protein   37.1g carbs   6.4g fibre

Deep green kale paired with chorizo is a winning combination making for a delicious, warming and filling soup.

Serves 6

* 3 tbsp olive oil
* 1 Spanish onion, finely chopped
* 2 garlic cloves, finely chopped
* 900 g/2 lb potatoes, diced
* 1.5 litres/2¾ pints vegetable stock
* 125 g/4½ oz chorizo or other spicy sausage, thinly sliced
* 450 g/1 lb kale or Savoy cabbage, cored and shredded
* salt and pepper (optional)

Time to get started

Heat 2 tablespoons of the oil in a large saucepan. Add the onion and garlic and cook over a low heat, stirring occasionally, for 5 minutes, until softened. Add the potatoes and cook, stirring constantly, for a further 3 minutes.

Increase the heat to medium, pour in the stock and bring to the boil. Reduce the heat, cover and cook for 10 minutes.

Meanwhile, heat the remaining oil in a frying pan. Add the chorizo and cook over a low heat, turning occasionally, for a few minutes, until the fat runs. Remove with a slotted spoon and drain on kitchen paper.

Remove the pan of soup from the heat and mash the potatoes with a potato masher. Return to the heat, add the kale and bring back to the boil. Reduce the heat and simmer for 5–6 minutes, until tender.

Remove the pan from the heat and mash the potatoes again. Stir in the chorizo and season to taste with salt and pepper, if using. Ladle into warmed bowls and serve immediately.

Green leaves

While many of us, especially kids may try and avoid eating green leafy vegetables they really are good for us. Choose from kale, purple sprouting broccoli, regular broccoli, Brussel sprouts, spinach and chard. The deeper the green, the more lutein and zeaxanthin, two cancer fighting antioxidants they contain which may also help reduce the risk of age-related macular degeneration too. Broccoli is also rich in sulphurous compounds and like antioxidants may also help protect against cancer. Plus they are also rich in B vitamins, and a good source of folic acid, important during pregnancy, immune boosting vitamin C and vitamin K for blood clotting.

Turkey soup with multigrains

Per serving: 388 cals 9.9g fat 1.9g sat fat 30.6g protein 45.5g carbs 8.9g fibre

Small steps make a big difference when eating healthily. Eating more wholegrains helps to lower cholesterol as they are high in soluble fibre, aiding good heart health.

Serves 4

* 85 g/3 oz aduki beans, soaked overnight in cold water
* 85 g/3 oz oat groats
* 55 g/2 oz freekeh
* 1 tbsp olive oil
* 150 g/5½ oz leeks, green and white parts separated and thinly sliced
* 250 g/9 oz turkey breast meat, diced
* 1.2 litres/2 pints chicken stock
* 20 g/¾ oz fresh ginger, peeled and chopped
* 150 g/5½ oz frozen soya beans
* 85 g/3 oz baby spinach leaves
* juice of 1 lemon
* salt and pepper (optional)

Meal in a bowl

Half fill a medium-sized saucepan with water, bring to the boil, then add the drained beans, the oat groats and the freekeh. Bring back to the boil and boil briskly for 10 minutes.

Meanwhile, heat the oil in a second saucepan, add the white leek slices and the turkey breast and fry over a medium heat, stirring, for 5 minutes until just beginning to colour.

Pour the stock into the turkey pan, then add the ginger. Drain the partly cooked grains, add to the pan, then bring to the boil, stirring. Cover and simmer for 25 minutes.

Add the soya beans, spinach and green leek slices. Cover and simmer for 5 minutes. Stir in the lemon juice, then add salt and pepper to taste, if using. Ladle into warmed shallow bowls and serve immediately.

Going with the grain

Eating more wholegrains helps to lower cholesterol as they are high in soluble fibre, aiding good heart health. As they take longer for the body to digest they also leave you feeling fuller for longer and give a slow and sustained energy release.

Asparagus & crab soup

Per serving: 95 cals   0.9g fat   0.2g sat fat   16.1g protein   5.6g carbs   1g fibre

Don't be put off by making your own stock, this version is easy but if you prefer, simply use a shop-bought chicken stock instead.

Serves 6

* 450 g/1 lb cooked fresh crabmeat
* 270 g/9½ oz fresh white or green asparagus, cut into 2-cm/¾-inch pieces
* 2 large egg whites, lightly beaten
* 1 tbsp cornflour
* 2 tbsp water
* salt and pepper (optional)
* 8 g/⅙ oz fresh coriander leaves, to garnish

Crab stock

* 2.8 litres/5 pints water
* 900 g/2 lb crab shells
* 25 g/1 oz fresh ginger, peeled and thinly sliced
* 4 spring onions, trimmed and crushed
* 2–3 tbsp nam pla (fish sauce)

Create your soup

For the stock, put the water and crab shells in a large saucepan and bring to the boil over a high heat. Reduce the heat to medium-low and add the ginger, spring onions and nam pla, then simmer for 1½ hours, or until reduced by about half, skimming off any froth. Strain the stock, discarding the solids, and remove any fat.

Pour the stock into a medium saucepan and bring to a gentle boil over a medium heat. Reduce the heat to medium-low, then add the crabmeat and asparagus, and season to taste with salt and pepper, if using. Cover and simmer for 5 minutes, or until the flavours have blended.

Steadily pour the egg whites into the soup, stirring a few times, and simmer for a further 1–2 minutes, or until fully cooked. In a ladle, stir the cornflour and water together. Lower the ladle into the soup, then stir a few times. Cook until lightly thickened.

Ladle the soup into warmed bowls and scatter over the coriander to garnish. Serve immediately.

Spring in your step

Spring onions are a rich source of cleansing sulphur that has multiple detoxifying effects. Spring onions also contain much more vitamin K than normal white onions, and this is needed along with phosphorus content to allow calcium to form new bone in babies in the womb.

Spicy peanut soup

Per serving: 403 cals   27.8g fat   10.4g sat fat   10.8g protein   34.1g carbs   5.4g fibre

This spicy and satisfying soup gets rich flavour from the peanut butter and a kick from the herbs and chillies.

Serves 4

* 1 tbsp vegetable oil
* 1 small onion, chopped
* 1 tbsp finely chopped fresh ginger
* 2 garlic cloves, finely chopped
* ½ tsp ground cumin
* ½ tsp pepper
* ¼ tsp ground cinnamon
* ¼ tsp cayenne pepper
* ¼ tsp turmeric
* 1½ tsp salt
* 2–4 serrano chillies, finely chopped
* 350 g/12 oz sweet potatoes, peeled and diced
* 700 ml/1¼ pints vegetable stock
* 400 g/14 oz canned chopped tomatoes, with their can juices
* 125 g/4½ oz smooth peanut butter
* 125 ml/4 fl oz coconut milk
* juice of 1 lemon
* 2 tbsp chopped fresh coriander leaves
* 2 spring onions, thinly sliced, and 4 fresh coriander sprigs, to garnish (optional)

Time to get started

Heat the oil in a medium-sized saucepan over a medium heat. Add the onion and cook, stirring frequently, for 10 minutes until soft. Stir in the ginger, garlic, cumin, pepper, cinnamon, cayenne pepper, turmeric and salt.

Add the chillies, sweet potatoes and stock and increase the heat to medium-high. Bring the mixture to the boil, then reduce the heat to medium-low and simmer for 20 minutes until the sweet potatoes are tender.

Add the tomatoes with their can juices and the peanut butter. Purée the soup in a blender. Return the soup to the pan and stir in the coconut milk, lemon juice and coriander. Gently cook over a medium heat until heated through. Ladle into warmed bowls and serve immediately, garnished with the spring onions and chopped coriander, if using.

Sweet potato & apple soup

Per serving: 291 cals   9.7g fat   5.8g sat fat   4.4g protein   48.2g carbs   6.9g fibre

A fantastically different recipe, this soup creates a whole new flavour combination to introduce to your taste buds.

Serves 6

* 1 tbsp butter
* 3 leeks, thinly sliced
* 1 large carrot, thinly sliced
* 600 g/1 lb 5 oz sweet potatoes, diced
* 2 large Bramley apples, peeled, cored and diced
* 1.2 litres/2 pints water
* ¼ tsp freshly grated nutmeg, or to taste
* 225 ml/8 fl oz apple juice
* 225 ml/8 fl oz single cream
* salt and pepper (optional)
* 2 tbsp snipped fresh chives or coriander, to garnish

Blend it

Melt the butter in a large saucepan over a medium-low heat.

Add the leeks, cover and cook for 6–8 minutes, or until soft, stirring frequently.

Add the carrot, sweet potatoes, apples and water. Lightly season to taste with salt and pepper, if using, and add the nutmeg. Bring to the boil, reduce the heat and simmer, covered, for about 20 minutes, stirring occasionally, until the vegetables are very tender.

Leave the soup to cool slightly, then purée in the pan with a hand-held blender.

Stir in the apple juice, place over a low heat and simmer for about 10 minutes, until heated through.

Stir in the cream and simmer for a further 5 minutes, stirring frequently, until heated through. Taste and adjust the seasoning, if necessary.

Ladle the soup into warmed bowls, garnish with chives and serve immediately.

Sweet stuff

Sweet potatoes are richer in nutrients than potatoes and lower on the glycaemic index, and so are of benefit for diabetics and dieters and for regulating blood sugar levels. They are also extremely high in beta-carotene as well as being an excellent source of vitamin E, magnesium and selenium.

Seared scallops in garlic broth

Per serving: 79 cals 3.7g fat 0.4g sat fat 7.2g protein 4.2g carbs 0.1g fibre

This is a truly special recipe, ideal for a special occasion as a show-stopping starter or the perfect pick-me-up treat on a cold day.

Serves 4

* 1 large garlic bulb (about 100 g/3½ oz), separated into unpeeled cloves
* 1 celery stick, chopped
* 1 carrot, chopped
* 1 onion, chopped
* 10 peppercorns
* 5–6 parsley sprigs
* 1.2 litres/2 pints water
* ¼ tsp salt, or to taste
* 225 g/8 oz large sea scallops or queen scallops
* 1 tbsp oil
* salt and pepper (optional)
* 12 fresh coriander leaves, to garnish

To make this soup

Combine the garlic cloves, celery, carrot, onion, peppercorns, parsley sprigs and water in a saucepan and add the salt, to taste. Bring to the boil, reduce the heat and simmer, partially covered, for 30–45 minutes.

Strain the stock into a clean saucepan and keep hot.

If using sea scallops, slice in half horizontally to form 2 thinner rounds from each. (If the scallops are very large, slice them into 3 rounds.) Sprinkle with salt and pepper, if using.

Heat the oil in a frying pan over a medium–high heat and cook the scallops on one side for 1–2 minutes, until lightly browned and the flesh becomes opaque.

Divide the scallops between 4 warmed shallow bowls, arranging them browned-side up. Ladle the soup over the scallops and garnish with fresh coriander leaves. Serve immediately.

Superb scallops

Scallops are a great source of vitamin B12, which is needed to deactivate homocysteine, a chemical that can damage blood vessel walls. A high intake of vitamin B12 has also been shown to protect against colon cancer.

Rejuvenate

Indian spiced cauliflower dhal soup

Per serving: 234 cals 6.5g fat 1.7g sat fat 12.8g protein 36.2g carbs 8.1g fibre

Cauliflower is stepping forward into the limelight. It's now thought this humble veg may help to fight cancer, boost heart health and act as an anti-inflammatory. Healthy eating needn't be expensive as this delicious soup proves.

Serves 4

* 1 tbsp sunflower oil
* 1 onion, finely chopped
* 1 cauliflower, cut into small florets
* 1 tsp coriander seeds, roughly crushed
* 1 tsp cumin seeds, roughly crushed
* 1 tsp black mustard seeds
* 1 tsp turmeric
* 1 litre/1¾ pints vegetable stock
* 150 g/5½ oz red lentils
* ¼ tsp salt
* large pinch of pepper
* 4 tbsp chopped fresh coriander

Time to get started

Heat the oil in a saucepan, add the onion and fry over a medium heat, stirring occasionally, for 5 minutes until soft. Add the cauliflower, coriander seeds, cumin seeds, black mustard seeds and turmeric, stir well to coat the cauliflower in the spices, then fry for 2–3 minutes until the cauliflower is coloured and just beginning to brown around the edges. Scoop out some of the cauliflower florets and reserve to garnish.

Pour the stock into the saucepan, add the lentils, salt and pepper and bring to the boil, stirring. Reduce the heat, cover and simmer for 30–35 minutes, stirring occasionally until the lentils are soft.

Roughly mash the soup, then stir in the chopped coriander. Ladle into warmed bowls, top with the reserved cauliflower florets and serve immediately.

Pork ramen soup

Per serving: 555 cals   11.8g fat   3.2g sat fat   44.5g protein   68.5g carbs   4.6g fibre

This ramen soup is delicious, filling and deeply satisfying. This classic version is garnished with slices of succulent barbecued pork fillet.

Serves 4

* 1 tbsp finely chopped fresh ginger
* 2 tbsp clear honey
* 2 tbsp soy sauce
* 2 tbsp mirin
* 1 tsp sesame oil
* 1 tsp Chinese five spice
* 1 pork fillet, about 675 g/1 lb 8 oz
* beansprouts, pea shoots and hard-boiled eggs, to garnish (optional)

Soup

* 1 tbsp vegetable oil
* 1 yellow onion, diced
* 3 garlic cloves, finely chopped
* 1 tbsp grated fresh ginger
* 1.5 litres/2¾ pints chicken stock
* 225 g/8 oz fresh shiitake mushrooms, stems removed and caps thinly sliced
* ½ tsp rock salt
* 4 tsp reduced-salt soy sauce
* 1 tablespoon Chinese rice wine
* 1 tsp sesame oil
* 500 g/1 lb 2 oz dried ramen noodles
* 4 tsp miso paste

Meal in a bowl

To prepare the pork, stir together the ginger, honey, soy sauce, mirin, sesame oil and five spice in a large bowl. Add the pork and turn to coat. Cover and refrigerate for at least 2 hours or overnight.

To make the soup, heat the vegetable oil in a large saucepan over a medium-high heat. Add the onion, garlic and ginger and cook, stirring, for 5 minutes, or until the onions are soft and translucent. Add the stock, mushrooms, salt, soy sauce, wine and sesame oil and bring to the boil. Reduce the heat to low and simmer, uncovered, for about 30 minutes.

Meanwhile, preheat the oven to 190°C/375°F/Gas Mark 5. Place the pork on a baking tray and roast in the preheated oven for 20 minutes.

Meanwhile, preheat a barbecue or grill to high. Transfer the pork to the grill rack and cook for about 5 minutes on each side, until brown and beginning to show grill marks. Reduce the heat to medium-low and continue to cook until a meat thermometer inserted into the thickest part of the meat registers a temperature of 63–68°C/145–155°F. Remove from the barbecue, loosely cover with foil, and leave to rest for 5 minutes before slicing.

Bring the soup back to the boil and add the noodles, breaking them up to ensure that they are all submerged in the liquid. Cook for about 3 minutes, until the noodles are tender. Stir in the miso paste until fully dissolved.

Thinly slice the pork. Ladle the soup into bowls, top with several slices of pork, garnish with the beansprouts, pea shoots and hard-boiled eggs and serve immediately.

Breton fish soup

Per serving: 401cals 24.1g fat 14.3g sat fat 18.3g protein 26.4g carbs 2.2g fibre

This rustic fisherman's soup is bursting with flavour and home comforts. Pairing chunky fish, potatoes, double cream and cider, it's hard to stop at just one bowl.

Serves 4

* 2 tsp butter
* 1 large leek, thinly sliced
* 2 shallots, finely chopped
* 125 ml/4 fl oz dry cider
* 300 ml/10 fl oz fish stock
* 250 g/9 oz potatoes, diced
* 1 bay leaf
* 4 tbsp plain flour
* 200 ml/7 fl oz milk
* 200 ml/7 fl oz double cream
* 55 g/2 oz fresh sorrel leaves
* 350 g/12 oz skinless monkfish or cod fillet, cut into 2.5-cm/1-inch pieces
* salt and pepper (optional)

How to make this soup

Melt the butter in a large saucepan over a medium-low heat. Add the leek and shallots and cook for about 5 minutes, stirring frequently, or until they start to soften. Add the cider and bring to the boil.

Stir in the stock, potatoes and bay leaf with a large pinch of salt (unless the stock is salty) and bring back to the boil. Reduce the heat, cover and cook gently for 10 minutes. Put the flour in a small bowl and very slowly whisk in a few tablespoons of the milk to make a thick paste. Stir in a little more milk to make a smooth liquid.

Adjust the heat so the soup bubbles gently. Stir in the flour mixture and cook, stirring frequently, for 5 minutes. Add the remaining milk and half of the cream. Continue cooking for about 10 minutes, or until the potatoes are tender.

Chop the sorrel finely and combine with the remaining cream. (If using a food processor, chop and add the sorrel, then add the cream and process briefly.)

Stir the sorrel cream into the soup and add the fish. Continue cooking, stirring occasionally, for about 3 minutes, or until the monkfish stiffens or the cod just begins to flake. Taste the soup and adjust the seasoning, if necessary. Remove and discard the bay leaf. Ladle into warmed bowls and serve immediately.

Roasted root soup with ginger & crème fraîche

Per serving: 401 cals   31.4g fat   8.6g sat fat   3.8g protein   29.6g carbs   5.3g fibre

A swirl of crème fraîche makes a healthy yet deliciously creamy addition to this gorgeous meat-free soup.

Serves 4

* 1 onion
* ½ small swede
* 1 sweet potato
* 2 carrots
* 1 potato
* 5 tbsp olive oil
* 2 tbsp tomato purée
* ¼ tsp pepper
* 2 large garlic cloves, peeled
* 2 tbsp groundnut oil
* 2 x 5-cm/2-inch pieces fresh ginger, peeled and sliced into thin shreds
* 850 ml/1½ pints hot vegetable stock
* ½ tsp sea salt
* 4 tbsp crème fraîche and 2 tbsp roughly chopped fresh flat-leaf parsley, to garnish

Time to get started

Preheat the oven to 190°C/375°F/Gas Mark 5. Cut the vegetables into large, even-sized chunks.

Mix the olive oil, tomato purée and pepper in a large bowl. Add the vegetables and the garlic and toss to coat.

Spread out the vegetables in a roasting tray. Roast in the preheated oven for 20 minutes, or until the garlic is soft. Remove the garlic and set aside. Roast the vegetables for a further 10–15 minutes, until tender.

Meanwhile, heat the groundnut oil in a frying pan over a high heat. Add the ginger and fry, turning constantly, for 1–2 minutes, until crisp.

Immediately remove the ginger from the pan and drain on kitchen paper. Set aside and keep warm.

Put the garlic and the other roasted vegetables into a food processor. Process in short bursts to a rough-textured purée.

Pour the purée into a saucepan and add the stock. Add the salt, then simmer, stirring, for 1–2 minutes, until heated through.

Ladle the soup into warmed bowls and swirl a tablespoon of crème fraîche into each.

Top with the sizzled ginger threads and chopped parsley and serve immediately.

Chicken & kimchi soup

Per serving: 184 cals 6.9g fat 1.9g sat fat 17g protein 13.6g carbs 2.8g fibre

Kimchi is a fermented vegetable pickle made with a variety of different vegetables. The pickle is thought to help promote the growth of healthy bacteria in the gut, which can become suppressed by a diet high in sugar and processed foods.

Serves 4

* 2 tsp rice bran oil
* 4 boneless, skinless chicken thighs, 300 g/10½ oz total weight
* 4 spring onions, thinly sliced
* 115 g/4 oz carrots, thinly sliced
* 1 red pepper, cored, deseeded and diced
* 850 ml/1½ pints chicken stock
* 1 tbsp brown rice miso
* 2 tbsp mirin
* 175 g/6 oz bottled kimchi, sliced, with the sauce clinging to the pickle

To make this soup

Heat the oil in a saucepan, then add the chicken and fry for 5 minutes until lightly browned on both sides. Add the spring onions, carrots and red pepper, then stir in the stock, miso and mirin.

Bring to the boil, then cover and simmer for 30 minutes until the rice is cooked through and there are no pink juices when the chicken is pierced in the thickest part with a knife. Lift the chicken out with a slotted spoon, then shred into strips using two forks.

Return the chicken to the soup and add the kimchi, then heat through, ladle into warmed bowls and serve immediately.

Creamy parsnip & cashew soup

Per serving: 399 cals 24.7g fat 4.2g sat fat 9.7g protein 40.4g carbs 9.7g fibre

A healthy alternative to potatoes, parsnips are often overlooked as a source of fibre and provide useful amounts of the antioxidant vitamins C and E. They are at their sweetest a few weeks after the first frost, making them a great winter vegetable.

Serves 4

* 140 g/5 oz cashew nut pieces
* 350 ml/12 fl oz cold water
* 1 tbsp sunflower oil
* 1 onion, finely chopped
* 1 garlic clove, finely chopped
* 4 tsp mild curry paste
* ¼ tsp turmeric
* 500 g/1 lb 2 oz parsnips, cubed
* 700 ml/1¼ pints vegetable stock
* 1 tbsp sunflower seeds
* 1 tbsp linseeds
* 1 tsp mild curry paste
* 1 tsp clear honey
* salt and pepper (optional)

Blend it

Put 115 g/4 oz of the cashew nuts into a bowl, cover with the water and leave to soak overnight. Next day add the nuts and soaking water to a blender and blitz until the nuts are coarsely ground. Tip into a sieve set over a bowl and leave the nut milk to drain.

Heat the oil in a saucepan, add the onion and fry over a medium heat for 5 minutes until soft. Stir in the garlic, curry paste, turmeric and drained chopped nuts and fry, stirring, for 3–4 minutes until the nuts are beginning to brown.

Stir the parsnips into the pan then pour in the stock and bring to the boil, stirring. Cover and simmer for 20 minutes until the parsnips are tender.

Meanwhile, dry-fry the remaining nuts, sunflower seeds and linseeds over a medium heat, stirring, for 3–5 minutes until the nuts are beginning to toast. Stir in the curry paste and honey and cook for 1 minute until the nuts and seeds are evenly coated and the honey is bubbling. Remove from the heat and leave to cool.

Purée the soup in batches in a blender until smooth. Return the soup to the pan, then mix in the cashew nut milk and reheat. Add salt and pepper to taste, if using. Ladle into warmed bowls, sprinkle with the nut and seed mix and serve immediately.

Chicken & kimchi soup

page 92

Creamy parsnip & cashew soup

page 93

Beef tom yum soup

A refreshing and reviving sweet-and-sour Thai broth that will awaken your senses and leave you feeling invigorated.

Serves 4

* 1½ tbsp sunflower oil
* 1 red onion, thinly sliced
* 3 tsp red Thai curry paste
* 1 tsp galangal paste
* 1 tsp palm sugar
* 2 kaffir lime leaves, halved
* 25 g/1 oz chopped fresh coriander
* 10 g/¼ oz fresh Thai basil, chopped
* 850 ml/1½ pints vegetable stock
* 250 g/9 oz rump steak, trimmed of fat
* 85 g/3 oz chestnut mushrooms, sliced
* 55 g/2 oz mangetout, halved
* 115 g/4 oz cherry tomatoes, halved
* ½ red pepper, cored, deseeded and cut into strips
* 1 lime, cut into wedges (optional)

Create your soup

Heat 1 tablespoon of the oil in a saucepan, add the onion and fry over a medium heat for 5 minutes until soft. Stir in the curry paste, galangal and sugar, then add the lime leaves, coriander, basil and stock. Bring to the boil, then cover and simmer for 5 minutes.

Heat a dry frying pan over a high heat, brush the steak with the remaining oil, then add to the pan and cook for 2 minutes on each side, or until cooked to your liking.

Add the mushrooms, mangetout, tomatoes and red pepper to the broth and cook for 3 minutes. Ladle into warmed bowls or layer in heatproof glasses. Cut the steak into thin strips and add to the broth. Serve immediately with lime wedges to squeeze over, if using.

Per serving: 174 cals 8.9g fat 2.1g sat fat 16.5g protein 9.8g carbs 1.8g fibre

Turkey miso soup

Per serving: 330 cals   10.5g fat   3.2g sat fat   27.4g protein   33.9g carbs   4.5g fibre

This comforting soup, enriched with miso paste, is just the thing to warm you up on a damp winter's day.

Serves 4

* 225 g/8 oz fresh udon noodles
* 1 tbsp vegetable oil
* 1 small leek, white and light green parts halved lengthways and thinly sliced
* 2.4 litres/4 pints turkey stock
* 3 carrots, sliced
* 1 tsp white pepper
* 225 g/8 oz sugar snap peas, halved
* 280 g/10 oz cooked turkey meat, shredded or chopped
* 4 tbsp white miso paste

Time to get started

Cook the noodles according to the packet instructions.

Heat the oil in a medium-sized saucepan over a medium-high heat. Add the leek and cook, stirring frequently, for 3 minutes, or until it begins to soften. Add the stock, carrots and pepper and bring to the boil. Reduce the heat to low and simmer for 15 minutes, or until the carrots are just tender.

Add the sugar snap peas, turkey and cooked noodles and simmer for 2–3 minutes until heated through. Stir in the miso paste until it is dissolved. Taste and adjust the seasoning if necessary.

Transfer the soup to warmed bowls and serve immediately.

Terrific turkey

Turkey is a high-protein alternative to chicken, with a rich, deep flavour. If you choose the dark meat (skin removed) rather than the pale breast meat, it contains a considerable amount more iron than chicken or pork.

Chicken & vegetable soup

Per serving: 263 cals   5.6g fat   1.9g sat fat   17.9g protein   37.9g carbs   6.5g fibre

A classic chicken and vegetable soup is always a welcome sight and smell and makes for a comforting meal any night of the week.

Serves 4

* 1 onion, finely chopped
* 1 garlic clove, finely chopped
* 115 g/4 oz white cabbage, shredded
* 2 medium carrots, finely chopped
* 4 potatoes, diced
* 1 green pepper, cored, deseeded and diced
* 400 g/14 oz canned chopped tomatoes
* 1.3 litres/2¼ pints chicken stock
* 175 g/6 oz cooked chicken, diced
* salt and pepper (optional)
* 2 tbsp chopped fresh flat-leaf parsley, to garnish

To make this soup

Put all the ingredients, except the chicken and parsley, in a large saucepan and bring to the boil. Simmer for 1 hour, or until the vegetables are tender.

Add the chicken and simmer for a further 10 minutes, or until hot.

Ladle the soup into warmed bowls and serve immediately, garnished with parsley.

Carotene carrots

Carrots are an excellent source of antioxidant compounds, and the richest vegetable source of carotenes, which give them their bright orange colour. These compounds help protect against cardiovascular disease and cancer, as well as promoting good vision and helping to maintain healthy lungs.

Manhattan clam chowder

Per serving: 322 cals 9.1g fat 3.1g sat fat 21.7g protein 32.4g carbs 4.7g fibre

This chowder has a relatively clear broth with the addition of tomatoes to add both flavour and a lovely, rich colour.

Serves 4

* 1 tsp sunflower oil
* 115 g/4 oz salt pork or unsmoked bacon, diced
* 1 onion, finely chopped
* 2 celery sticks, chopped
* 4 tomatoes, peeled, deseeded and chopped
* 3 potatoes, diced
* pinch of dried thyme
* 3 tbsp chopped fresh parsley
* 150 ml/5 fl oz tomato juice
* 600 ml/1 pint fish or vegetable stock
* 36 carpetshell or other small clams, scrubbed
* 150 ml/5 fl oz dry white wine
* salt and pepper (optional)
* crusty bread, to serve (optional)

Create your soup

Heat the oil in a saucepan. Add the salt pork and cook over a medium heat, stirring frequently, for 6-8 minutes, until golden brown. Remove with a slotted spoon.

Add the onion and celery to the pan, reduce the heat to low and cook, stirring occasionally, for 5 minutes, until softened. Increase the heat to medium and add the tomatoes, potatoes, thyme and parsley.

Return the pork to the pan, season to taste with salt and pepper, if using, and pour in the tomato juice and stock. Bring to the boil, stirring constantly, then reduce the heat, cover and simmer for 15-20 minutes, until the potatoes are just tender.

Meanwhile, discard any clams with broken shells and any that refuse to close when tapped. Put the remainder into a separate saucepan, pour in the wine, cover and cook over a high heat, shaking the pan occasionally, for 4-5 minutes, until the shells have opened.

Remove the clams with a slotted spoon and leave to cool slightly. Strain the cooking liquid through a muslin-lined strainer into the soup. Discard any clams that remain closed and remove the remainder from their shells.

Add the clams to the soup and heat through, stirring constantly, for 2-3 minutes. Remove from the heat and taste and adjust the seasoning, if necessary. Ladle into warmed bowls and serve immediately with crusty bread, if liked.

Wonton soup

Per serving: 160 cals 3.8g fat 1.3g sat fat 10.7g protein 21.4g carbs 0.7g fibre

If you're after a light soup that's still beautifully fragrant and flavourful, then try this deliciously delicate wonton soup.

Serves 6

* 175 g/6 oz minced chicken
* 55 g/2 oz cooked, peeled prawns, minced
* 1 spring onion, finely chopped
* 1 tsp finely chopped fresh ginger
* 1 tsp sugar
* 1 tbsp Chinese rice wine or dry sherry
* 2 tbsp light soy sauce
* 24 ready-made wonton wrappers
* 850 ml/1½ pints vegetable stock
* 2 tbsp snipped fresh chives, to garnish

Time to get started

Mix together the chicken, prawns, spring onion, ginger, sugar, rice wine and half the soy sauce in a bowl until thoroughly combined. Cover and leave to marinate for 20 minutes.

Put 1 teaspoon of the mixture in the centre of each wonton wrapper. Dampen the edges, fold corner to corner into a triangle and press to seal, then seal the bottom corners together.

Bring the stock to the boil in a large saucepan. Add the wontons and cook for 5 minutes. Stir in the remaining soy sauce and remove from the heat. Ladle the soup and wontons into warmed bowls, sprinkle with snipped chives and serve immediately.

Chicken tonight

Skinless chicken is a very low-fat source of protein, especially the light breast meat. Of the fat chicken does contain, almost half is monounsaturated and only a quarter is saturated, making it a great healthy choice.

Italian chicken soup with Parmesan

Per serving: 289 cals   10.7g fat   3.2g sat fat   25.9g protein   25.5g carbs   5.7g fibre

We should all be eating at least five portions of fruit and vegetables a day. Soup is a great way to add a range of healthy antioxidant-boosting vegetables into one vitamin-, mineral- and fibre-boosting meal.

Serves 4

* 1 tbsp olive oil
* 350 g/12 oz boneless, skinless chicken thighs, diced
* 1 onion, chopped
* 2 garlic cloves, finely chopped
* ½ red pepper, cored, deseeded and diced
* ½ orange pepper, cored, deseeded and diced
* 450 g/1 lb tomatoes, peeled and chopped
* 700 ml/1¼ pints chicken stock
* 55 g/2 oz wholemeal spaghetti, broken into small pieces
* 175 g/6 oz cauliflower, cut into small florets
* 85 g/3 oz tender stem broccoli, stems sliced and florets halved
* 55 g/2 oz kale, thinly shredded
* 15 g/½ oz basil leaves, torn
* 30 g/1 oz freshly grated Parmesan cheese
* salt and pepper (optional)

Meal in a bowl

Heat the oil in a large saucepan, add the chicken and fry over a medium heat, stirring, for 5 minutes until just beginning to brown. Stir in the onion and cook, stirring, for 5 minutes until the onion is just beginning to colour.

Mix in the garlic, red pepper, orange pepper and tomatoes. Cook for 2 minutes, then pour in the stock and bring to the boil. Cover and simmer for 40 minutes, stirring occasionally.

Add the spaghetti, cauliflower, broccoli and kale and simmer for 5 minutes until the spaghetti is tender but still firm to the bite. Add the basil leaves and salt and pepper to taste, if using. Ladle into warmed bowls, top with the cheese and serve immediately.

Lamb pepperpot soup

Per serving: 302 cals   10.1g fat   3g sat fat   22.8g protein   32g carbs   4.6g fibre

Boost flagging energy levels and spirits with this sustaining and chunky soup made with antioxidant-rich butternut squash, colourful red and yellow peppers, cholesterol-lowering farro and protein-rich, lean lamb fillet.

Serves 4

* 1 tbsp olive oil
* 350 g/12 oz neck of lamb fillet, diced
* 1 onion, chopped
* 350 g/12 oz butternut squash, peeled, deseeded and diced
* ½ red pepper, cored, deseeded and diced
* ½ yellow pepper, cored, deseeded and diced
* 1 tsp ground cumin
* 1 tsp ground coriander
* 1 tsp turmeric
* 850 ml/1½ pints lamb stock
* 1 tbsp tomato purée
* 85 g/3 oz quick-cook farro
* salt and pepper (optional)

How to make it

Heat the oil in a medium-sized saucepan, then add the lamb and cook over a medium heat, stirring, for 5 minutes until brown. Add the onion and fry for 5 minutes until lightly coloured.

Add the squash, red pepper and yellow pepper, then mix in the cumin, coriander and turmeric. Pour in the stock, add the tomato purée and farro and bring to the boil, stirring.

Cover and simmer for 30 minutes until the lamb is tender. Add salt and pepper to taste, if using. Ladle into warmed bowls and serve immediately.

Italian chicken soup with Parmesan

page 104

Lamb pepperpot soup

page 105

Prawn & fermented black bean soup

This wonderfully colourful soup is like a rainbow in a bowl. Low in fat, it is packed with protein, immune system-boosting vitamins and minerals, the body's defence team.

Serves 4

* 1 litre/1¾ pints vegetable stock
* 1 tbsp fermented black bean paste
* 25 g/1 oz fresh ginger, peeled and finely chopped
* 1 kaffir lime leaf
* 4 spring onions, thinly sliced
* 2 tsp tamari
* 2 tsp clear honey
* 250 g/9 oz frozen cooked peeled tiger prawns, thawed, rinsed and drained
* 115 g/4 oz frozen edamame beans
* 115 g/4 oz baby corn, sliced
* 70 g/2½ oz young white, green or rainbow Swiss chard leaves
* 20 g/¾ oz chopped fresh coriander
* 2 tsp sesame seeds, toasted

Create your soup

Add the stock, bean paste, ginger, lime leaf and spring onions to a medium-sized saucepan. Stir in the tamari and honey and bring to the boil, then cover and simmer for 5 minutes.

Add the prawns and beans and cook for 3 minutes, then add the baby corn and chard. Cook for 2 minutes until the chard has just wilted and the prawns are piping hot.

Stir in the coriander and sprinkle with the sesame seeds. Ladle into warmed bowls and serve immediately.

Per serving: 169 cals   4.7g fat   1.4g sat fat   21.3g protein   11.7g carbs   3.3g fibre

Roast mushroom & garlic soup with wholemeal croûtons

Per serving: 217 cals 8.5g fat 2g sat fat 10.8g protein 30.4g carbs 5.5g fibre

Large meaty mushrooms make this soup a real winner when you're feeling hungry but don't fancy a meat-based meal.

Serves 1

* 2 open-cap mushrooms, wiped clean
* 2 garlic cloves, peeled
* 1 slice wholemeal bread, cut into small cubes
* 5 ml/1 tsp olive oil
* 10 g/¼ oz dried porcini mushrooms
* 250 ml/9 fl oz vegetable stock
* 1 tsp fresh thyme leaves
* 5 ml/1 tsp Worcestershire sauce
* 1 tsp half-fat crème fraîche (optional)
* freshly ground black pepper (optional)
* 1 sprig of thyme, to garnish

How to make it

Preheat the oven to 180°C/350°F/Gas Mark 4.

Loosely wrap the open-cap mushrooms and garlic in foil and place in the preheated oven. Bake for 10 minutes, open the foil, and bake for a further 5 minutes.

To prepare the croûtons, drizzle the bread cubes with 1 teaspoon of olive oil, place on a baking sheet and bake for 10–15 minutes or until golden brown.

Meanwhile, put the porcini mushrooms, stock and thyme leaves in a lidded saucepan.

When the open-cap mushrooms are cooked, remove from the oven, slice and add them to the saucepan with the Worcestershire sauce, roasted garlic, the mushroom juices and pepper, if using.

Cover and simmer for 15 minutes over a low heat.

Leave to cool slightly and purée half the soup in an electric blender for a few seconds. Return to the pan and reheat gently. Stir in the crème fraîche, if using, and adjust the pepper to taste, if necessary.

Transfer to a warmed bowl, sprinkle over the croûtons and sprig of thyme and serve immediately.

Lemon, chicken & rice soup

Per serving: 345 cals   8.3g fat   2.3g sat fat   32.5g protein   35.6g carbs   4.1g fibre

This is a hearty soup with a beautifully balanced range of ingredients. The added cheesy twist of a Parmesan garnish is by no means necessary as it works perfectly well on its own.

Serves 4

* 1 onion
* 1 leek
* 1 garlic clove
* 1 tbsp vegetable oil
* finely grated zest and juice of ½ lemon
* 100 g/3½ oz basmati rice
* 1 litre/1¾ pints chicken stock
* 2 cooked chicken breasts
* 100 g/3½ oz fresh spinach
* 175 g/6 oz frozen peas
* 4 tbsp chopped fresh flat-leaf parsley
* salt and pepper (optional)
* Parmesan cheese shavings, to garnish (optional)

Meal in a bowl

Finely chop the onion and leek and crush the garlic. Heat the oil in a large saucepan over a medium heat. Add the onion and leek and sauté for 4–5 minutes, until starting to soften. Add the garlic and lemon zest and cook for a further 1–2 minutes.

Add the rice and stock and bring to the boil. Cover and simmer for 8 minutes. Roughly chop the chicken, add to the pan with the spinach and peas and season to taste with salt and pepper, if using. Cook for a further 4 minutes, or until the rice is cooked through.

Stir in the lemon juice and parsley and transfer to warmed bowls. Shave the Parmesan over, if liked, and serve immediately.

Luscious lemons

All parts of the lemon contain valuable nutrients and antioxidants. They are a particularly good source of vitamin C. The plant compound antioxidants include limonene, an oil that may help to prevent breast and other cancers and lower 'bad' cholesterol, and rutin, which has been found to strengthen veins.

Cauliflower

This rather forgotten vegetable is now seeing a revival, it is part of the cruciferous family of vegetables which includes dark green kale and broccoli. Snowy white cauliflower with its milky almost nutty flavour contains a large range of nutrients. Rich in antioxidants and phytonutrients thought to help protect against cancer; minerals and B vitamins including choline, essential for learning and memory; immune boosting vitamin C and vitamin K, known for blood clotting and to aid heart health, it is also thought to improve bone health. Low in calories too, so you can eat generous portions, either raw, cooked and mashed as a low calorie alternative to mashed potatoes or added to soups, stews and curries.

Crab & vegetable soup

Per serving: 266 cals   14.8g fat   7g sat fat   18.5g protein   16.6g carbs   2.7g fibre

Save this soup for a celebration as it will offer a real wow-factor as well as a truly special taste sensation.

Serves 4

* 2 tbsp chilli oil
* 1 garlic clove, chopped
* 4 spring onions, trimmed and sliced
* 2 red peppers, deseeded and chopped
* 1 tbsp grated fresh ginger
* 1 litre/1¾ pints fish stock
* 100 ml/3½ fl oz coconut milk
* 100 ml/3½ fl oz rice wine or sherry
* 2 tbsp lime juice
* 1 tbsp grated lime rind
* 6 kaffir lime leaves, finely shredded
* 300 g/10½ oz freshly cooked crabmeat
* 200 g/7 oz freshly cooked crab claws
* 150 g/5½ oz canned sweetcorn, drained
* 1 tbsp chopped coriander, plus 1 tbsp, to garnish
* salt and pepper (optional)

Create your soup

Heat the oil in a large saucepan over a medium heat. Add the garlic and spring onions and cook, stirring, for about 3 minutes, until slightly softened. Add the red peppers and ginger and cook for a further 4 minutes, stirring.

Pour in the stock and season to taste with salt and pepper, if using. Bring to the boil, then lower the heat. Pour in the coconut milk, rice wine and lime juice, and stir in the grated lime rind and kaffir lime leaves. Simmer for 15 minutes.

Add the crabmeat and crab claws to the soup with the sweetcorn and coriander. Cook the soup for 5 minutes until the crab is heated right through.

Remove from the heat. Ladle into warmed bowls, garnish with coriander and serve immediately.

Don't get crabby

Crabs are low in total fat and saturates and rich in minerals. Crabmeat is a good source of l-tyrosine, an amino acid that has been shown to help brain power. It contains as much protein as a similar weight of lean beef and is therefore ideal for vegetarians who eat fish and seafood.

Detox

Miso soup

Per serving: 71 cals   2.4g fat   0.4g sat fat   5.2g protein   7.1g carbs   0.7g fibre

Miso is one of the traditional foods of Japan. This soup is simplicity at its best and is both quick to prepare and cook making it the perfect healthy fast food.

Serves 4

* 1 litre/1¾ pints water
* 2 tsp dashi granules
* 175 g/6 oz silken tofu, drained and cut into small cubes
* 4 shiitake mushrooms, finely sliced
* 4 tbsp miso paste
* 2 spring onions, chopped

Create your soup

Put the water in a large pan with the dashi granules and bring to the boil. Add the tofu and mushrooms, reduce the heat, and let it simmer for 3 minutes.

Stir in the miso paste and let it simmer gently, stirring, until the miso has dissolved.

Add the spring onions and serve immediately in warmed bowls. If you leave the soup, the miso will settle, so stir before serving to recombine.

Miso hungry

Miso is associated with good gut health because it feeds the beneficial probiotic bacteria present in the body. This supports toxin elimination and the absorption of nutrients to keep you looking and feeling young and healthy.

Pea, broccoli & wheatgrass soup

Per serving: 229 cals 7.8g fat 1.3g sat fat 8.9g protein 33.6g carbs 10.3g fibre

Enhance this soup and boost your nutrition levels even higher with a spoonful of vitamin- and mineral-rich powdered wheatgrass in this soothing, nutrient-boosting, vibrant and fresh-tasting dish.

Serves 4

* 1 tbsp olive oil
* 4 spring onions, sliced
* 1 dessert apple, cored and diced
* 300 g/10½ oz broccoli, stem sliced and florets cut into small pieces
* 600 ml/1 pint vegetable stock
* 250 g/9 oz frozen peas
* 4 tsp wheatgrass powder
* 300 ml/10 fl oz unsweetened rice milk
* 2 tbsp chia seeds
* pepper (optional)

Blend it

Heat the oil in a saucepan, add the spring onions, apple and broccoli stems and fry over a medium heat for 3–4 minutes until soft. Pour in the stock and bring to the boil, then cover and simmer for 10 minutes until the broccoli stems are just tender.

Add the broccoli florets and peas and stir well, then re-cover the pan and cook for 5 minutes until the vegetables are just tender and bright green.

Purée the vegetables and stock in a blender or food processor with the wheatgrass powder. Return to the pan and stir in the rice milk and chia seeds. Bring to the boil, stirring, then add a little pepper to taste, if using. Ladle into warmed bowls or mugs and serve immediately.

Chia cheer!

Chia seeds may be tiny but these almost tasteless black seeds provide valuable protein, fibre, omega 3 and omega 6 essential fatty acids plus a range of minerals.

Radish, lettuce & wasabi soup

Per serving: 76 cals 5.5g fat 1.2g sat fat 1.6g protein 6g carbs 2.8g fibre

Delicately flavoured with just a hint of wasabi, this mooli and red radish soup is light and fresh, with just a hint of green from shredded Little Gem lettuces. It's the perfect antidote to heavy and meaty winter dishes.

Serves 4

* 1 tbsp rice bran oil
* 4 spring onions, chopped
* 200 g/7 oz mooli, peeled and coarsely grated
* 115 g/4 oz red radishes, thinly sliced
* 2-cm/¾-inch piece fresh ginger, peeled and coarsely grated
* 450 ml/15 fl oz vegetable stock
* 1 tsp wasabi powder
* 450 ml/15 fl oz unsweetened almond milk
* 1 Little Gem lettuce, thinly shredded

Time to get started

Heat the oil in a saucepan, add the spring onions and fry over a medium heat for 3 minutes until soft. Add the mooli, red radishes and ginger and cook, stirring, for a further 2 minutes.

Pour in the stock, bring to the boil, stirring, then cover and simmer for 10 minutes.

Mix the wasabi to a smooth paste with a little water, then stir into the soup with the almond milk and lettuce. Bring back to the boil and cook for 1 minute until the lettuce has just wilted.

Ladle the soup into warmed bowls or pour the liquid and two thirds of the vegetables into a blender or food processor and purée until smooth. Reheat if needed, then ladle into warmed bowls, top with the remaining vegetables and serve immediately.

Pea, broccoli &
wheatgrass soup

page 120

Radish, lettuce &
wasabi soup

page 121

Shiitake mushroom & seaweed soup

Dried seaweed is rich in vitamins A and K and folates, with a magnesium and calcium content but also contains a staggering ten times more iodine than any other food.

Serves 4

* 5-cm/2-inch piece dried kombu seaweed
* 850 ml/1½ pints cold vegetable stock
* 1 tbsp rice bran oil
* 115 g/4 oz shiitake mushrooms, sliced
* 85 g/3 oz green leek tops, thinly sliced
* 25 g/1 oz fresh ginger, peeled, sliced and cut into thin strips
* 10 g/¼ oz dried dulse, thinly shredded
* 55 g/2 oz kale, thinly shredded
* 25 g/1 oz chopped fresh coriander
* 1 tbsp brown rice vinegar
* 2 tsp tamari

How to make it

Put the kombu into a bowl with 300 ml/10 fl oz of the stock and leave to soak for 20 minutes.

Heat the oil in a medium-sized saucepan, add the mushrooms and leeks and cook over a medium heat, stirring, for 5 minutes until soft.

Add the kombu and soaking liquid to the mushrooms, then pour in the remaining stock and add the ginger. Bring to the boil, then cover and simmer for 5 minutes.

Add the dulse, kale and coriander, then stir in the vinegar and tamari. Cook gently for 5 minutes. Remove the kombu from the pan, then ladle the soup into warmed bowls and serve immediately.

Per serving: 93 cals   5.1g fat   1.5g sat fat   3g protein   11.8g carbs   3.1g fibre

Spicy lentil soup

Per serving: 289 cals 8g fat 1.4g sat fat 14g protein 42.4g carbs 10.2g fibre

Lentils don't require soaking before cooking, making them much quicker and easier to use than other pulses.

Serves 4

* 1 litre/1¾ pints water
* 250 g/9 oz toor dahl or chana dahl
* 1 tsp paprika
* ½ tsp chilli powder
* ½ tsp ground turmeric
* 2 tbsp ghee or vegetable oil
* 1 fresh green chilli, deseeded and finely chopped
* 1 tsp cumin seeds
* 3 curry leaves, roughly torn
* 1 tsp sugar
* salt (optional)
* 1 tsp garam masala, to garnish

Time to get started

Bring the water to the boil in a large, heavy-based saucepan. Add the dahl, cover and simmer, stirring occasionally, for 25 minutes.

Stir in the paprika, chilli powder and turmeric, re-cover and cook for a further 10 minutes, or until the dahl is tender.

Meanwhile, heat the ghee in a small frying pan. Add the chilli, cumin seeds and curry leaves and cook, stirring constantly, for 1 minute.

Add the spice mixture to the dahl. Stir in the sugar and season to taste with salt, if using. Ladle into warmed bowls, garnish with garam masala and serve immediately.

Love your lentils

Lentils are a very rich source of fibre, both insoluble and soluble, which helps protect us against cancer and cardiovascular disease. Lentils are also rich in B vitamins, folate and all major minerals, particularly iron and zinc.

Pumpkin & haricot bean soup

Per serving: 134 cals 3.2g fat 1.1g sat fat 7.2g protein 20.2g carbs 6.3g fibre

A hearty warming soup on a cold day, this soup will satisfy your taste buds and also leave you feeling nicely full.

Serves 4

* 1 tsp olive oil
* 1 red onion, chopped
* 2 garlic cloves, crushed
* 450 g/1 lb pumpkin, peeled, deseeded and chopped into small cubes
* 2 tsp smoked paprika
* ¼ tsp dried chilli flakes
* 5-6 fresh sage leaves, finely chopped
* 850 ml/1½ pints gluten-free vegetable stock
* 400 g/14 oz canned haricot beans, drained and rinsed
* salt and pepper (optional)
* 2 tbsp finely chopped, fresh flat-leaf parsley, to garnish

Meal in a bowl

Heat the oil in a saucepan and fry the onion and garlic for 3-4 minutes. Add the pumpkin and cook for a further 4-5 minutes.

Add the paprika, chilli and sage and cook for 1 minute, stirring all the time.

Pour in the stock and season to taste with salt and pepper, if using. Cover and simmer for 20-25 minutes, or until the pumpkin is tender. Allow the soup to cool slightly then process, using a hand-held blender, until smooth.

Stir in the haricot beans and heat through for 2-3 minutes. Ladle into warmed bowls, garnish with the parsley and serve immediately.

Sacred sage

Sage is one of the highest plants on the ORAC scale, with a rating of 32,004 when fresh and 119,929 when dried. As such, sage is a powerful weapon against the free radicals that contribute to the ageing process, as it is able to neutralize them before they can damage body cells.

Keen green soup

Per serving: 26 cals   0.2g fat   trace sat fat   0.9g protein   3.4g carbs   1.3g fibre

This simple yet invigorating soup with refreshing cucumber and plenty of chilled water will cool you down on a hot day.

Serves 2

* 180 g/6 ¼ oz cucumber
* 2 celery sticks
* 2 tbsp chopped fresh parsley, plus 2 extra sprigs, to garnish
* 2 tbsp chopped fresh mint
* 2 tbsp chopped fresh coriander
* 250 ml/9 fl oz chilled water

Blend it

Chop the cucumber and celery and add to a blender with the parsley, mint, coriander and water. Blend until smooth.

Serve immediately or chill in the refrigerator and stir just before serving, garnished with parsley.

Cool as a cucumber

There is some evidence that cucumber can help to build and maintain healthy connective tissue – ligaments and cartilage in our body – as we age. This is mainly because it is a good source of the mineral silica, which is an essential component of this tissue, as well as of bone and muscle.

Carrot & lentil soup

Per serving: 322 cals   12.8g fat   4.2g sat fat   13.1g protein   43.1g carbs   7.4g fibre

Carrots and lentils make a great pairing, balancing the nutty taste of the lentils with the sweetness of carrots.

Serves 4

* 125 g/4½ oz split red lentils
* 1.2 litres/2 pints vegetable stock
* 350 g/12 oz carrots, sliced
* 2 onions, chopped
* 225 g/8 oz canned chopped tomatoes
* 2 garlic cloves, chopped
* 2 tbsp ghee or oil
* 1 tsp ground cumin
* 1 tsp ground coriander
* 1 fresh green chilli, deseeded and chopped
* ½ tsp ground turmeric
* 1 tbsp lemon juice
* 300 ml/10 fl oz milk
* 2 tbsp chopped fresh coriander
* salt (optional)
* 4 tbsp natural yogurt, to serve

How to make it

Place the lentils in a large saucepan, together with 900 ml/1½ pints of the stock, the carrots, onions, tomatoes and garlic. Bring the mixture to the boil, then reduce the heat, cover and simmer for 30 minutes, or until the vegetables and lentils are tender.

Meanwhile, heat the ghee in a small saucepan. Add the cumin, ground coriander, chilli and turmeric and fry over a low heat for 1 minute. Remove from the heat and stir in the lemon juice. Season to taste with salt, if using.

Remove the soup from the heat and leave to cool slightly. Transfer to a food processor or blender, in batches if necessary, and process to a purée. Return the soup to the rinsed-out pan, add the spice mixture and the remaining stock and simmer over a low heat for 10 minutes.

Add the milk and taste and adjust the seasoning, if necessary. Stir in the chopped coriander and reheat gently. Ladle into warmed bowls, top each with a swirl of yogurt and serve immediately.

Vegetable pho

Per serving: 207 cals   2.8g fat   1.6g sat fat   5.8g protein   42.6g carbs   4.2g fibre

A spoon won't quite be sufficient to eat this wonderful soup which is laden with vegetables and noodles.

Serves 4

* 1.5 litres/2¾ pints vegetable stock
* 2 tbsp tamari
* 2 garlic cloves, thinly sliced
* 2.5-cm/1-inch piece ginger, peeled and thinly sliced
* 1 cinnamon stick
* 1 bay leaf
* 1 medium carrot, cut into thin batons
* 1 small fennel bulb, thinly sliced
* 150 g/5½ oz vermicelli rice noodles
* 85 g/3 oz button mushrooms, sliced
* 115 g/4 oz beansprouts
* 4 spring onions, thinly sliced diagonally
* 3 tbsp chopped fresh coriander
* fresh basil leaves, chopped red chillies, lime wedges and tamari, to serve (optional)

Create your soup

Place the stock in a large pan with the tamari, garlic, ginger, cinnamon and bay leaf. Bring to the boil, reduce the heat, cover and simmer for about 20 minutes.

Add the carrot and fennel and simmer for 1 minute. Add the noodles and simmer for a further 4 minutes.

Add the mushrooms, beansprouts and spring onions and return to the boil.

Ladle into warmed soup bowls and sprinkle with the coriander. Remove and discard the bay leaf. Serve immediately with basil leaves, chillies, lime wedges and tamari, if using.

Brilliant beansprouts

Beansprouts are ideal to help weight control as they are very low in calories and high in fibre. They are a very good source of pantothenic acid, a type of B vitamin, which may control depression.

Rocket fuel soup

Per serving: 420 cals   41.7g fat   25.7g sat fat   5.9g protein   14.1g carbs   7.8g fibre

The mild spice from the rocket and mustard leaves is softened by the avocado and coconut milk, creating a creamy but healthy soup.

Serves 1

* 20 g/¾ oz rocket, plus 10 g/¼ oz extra leaves, to garnish
* 20 g/¾ oz mustard leaves
* 200 ml/7 fl oz chilled water
* ½ avocado, stoned and flesh scooped from skin
* 125 ml/4 fl oz coconut milk

Blend it

Put the rocket, mustard leaves and water into a blender and blend until smooth.

Add the avocado flesh to the blender with the coconut milk and blend until smooth and creamy.

Serve immediately or chill in the refrigerator. Stir well just before serving, garnished with a few rocket leaves.

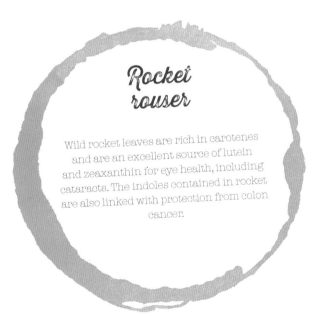

Rocket rouser

Wild rocket leaves are rich in carotenes and are an excellent source of lutein and zeaxanthin for eye health, including cataracts. The indoles contained in rocket are also linked with protection from colon cancer.

Borscht

Per serving: 359 cals   19.3g fat   11.8g sat fat   7.3g protein   45.6g carbs   11.4g fibre

It's hard to beat the magnificent ruby red colour of this European soup, particularly favoured in Russia, the Ukraine and Poland.

Serves 4

* 5 raw beetroot, about
  1 kg/2 lb 4 oz
* 70 g/2½ oz butter
* 2 onions, thinly sliced
* 3 carrots, thinly sliced
* 3 celery sticks, thinly sliced
* 6 tomatoes, peeled, deseeded and
  chopped
* 1 tbsp red wine vinegar
* 1 tbsp sugar
* 2 garlic cloves, finely chopped
* 1 bouquet garni
* 1.3 litres/2¼ pints
  vegetable stock
* salt and pepper (optional)
* 4 tbsp soured cream
* 2 tbsp chopped fresh dill,
  to garnish

To make this soup

Peel and coarsely grate four of the beetroot. Melt the butter in a large saucepan. Add the onions and cook over a low heat, stirring occasionally, for 5 minutes, until softened. Add the grated beetroot, carrots and celery, and cook, stirring occasionally, for a further 5 minutes.

Increase the heat to medium and add the tomatoes, vinegar, sugar, garlic and bouquet garni. Season to taste with salt and pepper, if using. Stir well, pour in the stock and bring to the boil. Reduce the heat, cover and simmer for 1¼ hours.

Meanwhile, peel and grate the remaining beetroot. Add it and any juices to the pan and simmer for a further 10 minutes. Remove the pan from the heat and leave to stand for 10 minutes.

Remove and discard the bouquet garni. Ladle the soup into warmed bowls and top each with a spoonful of soured cream. Garnish with dill and serve immediately.

Beautiful beetroot

Beetroot are rich in betaine – a compound that helps improve digestion and nutrient absorption, reducing bloating, calm food intolerances and control yeast and bacterial growth. The nitrates in the root can also raise HDL cholesterol, protect against blood clots and lower high blood pressure significantly for up to 24 hours.

Gingered beef tea

Per serving: 84 cals   2.5g fat   1g sat fat   29.2g protein   11g carbs   1.8g fibre

Beef tea or bone broth was a favourite home remedy from our grandmothers' time. Rich in minerals and vitamins it was served to convalescents to aid recovery and boost health.

Serves 4

* 2 kg/4 lb 8 oz beef bones, cut into large pieces
* 2 onions, cut into chunks
* 225 g/8 oz carrots, thickly sliced
* 4 celery sticks, thickly sliced
* 3 garlic cloves, halved
* 140 g/5 oz fresh ginger, unpeeled, thinly sliced
* 2 tbsp reduced-salt soy sauce
* 3 litres/5¼ pints water
* 1 tsp black peppercorns, roughly crushed
* 70 g/2½ oz fresh ginger, peeled and thinly sliced, to serve

How to make it

Preheat the oven to 220°C/425°F/Gas Mark 7. Put the beef bones into a large roasting tin and bake in the preheated oven for 30 minutes until just beginning to brown. Turn the bones over and add the onions, carrots, celery and garlic. Bake for about 30 minutes until the bones are deep brown and the vegetables are tinged with colour.

Scoop the bones and vegetables from the tin with a large slotted spoon, draining off as much fat as possible, and add to a large saucepan.

Add the unpeeled ginger and soy sauce, then pour over the water and mix in the peppercorns. Bring to the boil, skimming off any foam, then cover and simmer gently for 4 hours.

Pour the broth through a muslin-lined fine sieve into a large measuring jug. You should have about 1.4 litres/2½ pints. If you have a lot more, return it to the pan and simmer, uncovered, to reduce and concentrate the flavours.

Leave to cool, then chill overnight. Scoop the fat off the top with a spoon, then add the peeled ginger, place over a medium heat, bring to a simmer and gently simmer for 5 minutes. Ladle into warmed mugs and serve immediately.

Good to the bone!

Bone broth is helpful in treating digestive disorders such as IBS, colitis and even Crohn's disease.

Beetroot & cranberry broth

Per serving: 64 cals   1.6g fat   1g sat fat   1.6g protein   12.9g carbs   2.6g fibre

Beetroot contains most of the vitamins and minerals the body needs, while cranberries are great for bladder and kidney infections. The sweetness of the beetroot and sharpness of the cranberries make this soup a delicious natural pick-me-up.

Serves 4

* 500 g/1 lb 2 oz uncooked beetroot, peeled and diced
* 1 onion, finely chopped
* 115 g/4 oz fresh or frozen cranberries
* 1 litre/1¾ pints vegetable stock
* 2 tsp tomato purée
* 2 tsp dark muscovado sugar
* juice of 1 orange
* 70 g/2½ oz kimchi, thinly shredded

Time to get started

Put the beetroot, onion and cranberries into a saucepan, pour over the stock, then add the tomato purée and sugar. Bring to the boil, then cover and simmer for 30 minutes until the beetroot is tender and the cranberries are soft.

Tip into a large sieve set over a large jug to strain the broth. Divide one third of the beetroot mixture between four heatproof serving glasses, discarding the remainder. Stir the orange juice into the strained broth, pour into the glasses, top with the kimchi and serve immediately.

Gingered beef tea
page 138

Beetroot &
cranberry broth
page 139

Cleansing chicken & celery broth

Wonderfully comforting and reviving, this clear broth will settle and calm an anxious tummy, aid digestion and help reduce bloating. It is also a good source of antioxidants. For an extra boost of vitamin C you might like to squeeze in a little fresh lemon juice.

Serves 4

* 1 chicken carcass
* 1.5 litres/2¾ pints water
* 9 celery sticks, including leaves, 5 thickly sliced
* 175 g/6 oz leeks, thickly sliced
* 115 g/4 oz carrots, thickly sliced
* 25 g/1 oz fresh parsley sprigs
* pepper (optional)

Create your soup

Break the chicken carcass in half, place in a medium-sized saucepan and cover with the water. Add the sliced celery, leeks, carrots and parsley and bring to the boil, stirring. Cover and simmer for 1½ hours.

Strain the broth through a fine sieve into a jug, adding pepper to taste, if using, then pour into warmed mugs. Serve immediately with the celery sticks as stirrers.

Per serving: 21 cals   0.7g fat   0.1g sat fat   1g protein   3.9g carbs   0.9g fibre

Seaweed

Seaweed is one of the most nutritionally dense plants, so a little goes a long way. Choose from dulse, a red seaweed sold as dried shreds, soak before use and add to soups, salads or buy as dried flakes. Nori sheets are perhaps the most widely known, choose untoasted sheets if you can, use for sushi rolls or crumble and sprinkle over soups and salads. Arame, a black stringy seaweed is more difficult to find, again soak in cold water before use, add to salads and soups. Soak kombu and eat only the soaking water and not the seaweed itself.

Seaweed contains lignans which have anti-cancer properties, rich in calcium for bone strength, they help to neutralize acid effects of our modern diet, rich in chlorophyll, a powerful natural detoxifier. Best known for being high in iodine which helps to stimulate the thyroid gland, responsible for maintaining a healthy metabolism.

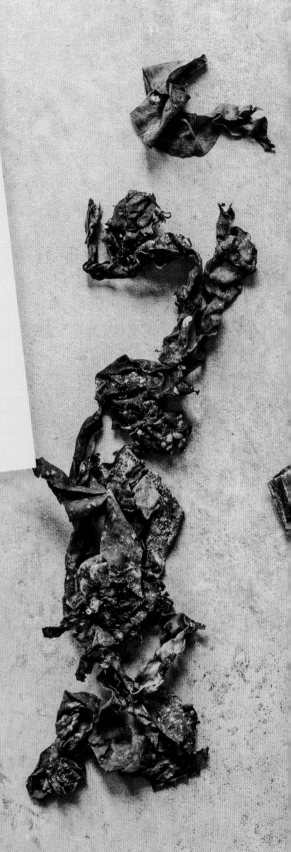

Melon breeze soup

Per serving: 192 cals   0.9g fat   0.2g sat fat   4g protein   46.6g carbs   5.2g fibre

Unlike winter soups, which warm your insides, this soup will cool you down and chill you out. Perfect for a summer starter or as part of your lunch.

Serves 1

* 300 g/10 ½ oz green melon, peeled and deseeded
* 250 g/9 oz cucumber
* 4 tbsp chopped fresh mint, plus a sprig to garnish
* 200 ml/7 fl oz chilled coconut water

Blend it

Chop the melon and cucumber and place in a blender.

Add the mint, pour over the coconut water and blend until smooth and creamy.

Serve immediately or chill in the refrigerator and stir just before serving, garnished with a sprig of mint.

Melon magic

A melon contains 92 per cent water which can help keep the kidneys working well. All melons are rich in vitamin B6, potassium and soluble fibre.

South Indian lentil broth

Per serving: 161 cals   7.6g fat   1.2g sat fat   5.9g protein   18.3g carbs   4.2g fibre

This is a wonderfully warming soup but also rather thin. You can choose to serve it with rice to make it a more substantial meal if you wish.

Serves 4

* 100 g/3½ oz pigeon peas (tuvar dal)
* 600 ml/1 pint cold water
* 1 tsp ground turmeric
* 2 tbsp vegetable or groundnut oil
* 1 tsp black mustard seeds
* 6-8 fresh curry leaves
* 1 tsp cumin seeds
* 1 fresh green chilli
* 1 tsp tamarind paste
* 1 tsp salt

How to make it

Rinse the pigeon peas under cold running water, then place in a saucepan with the water, turmeric and 1 tablespoon of the oil. Cover and simmer for 25-30 minutes, or until the lentils are cooked and tender.

Heat the remaining oil in a frying pan over a medium heat. Add the mustard seeds, curry leaves, cumin seeds, chilli and tamarind paste. When the seeds start to pop, remove the pan from the heat and add to the lentil mixture with the salt.

Return the broth to the heat for 2-3 minutes. Ladle into warmed bowls and serve immediately.

Tasty turmeric

Turmeric comes from the orange-fleshed root of a plant native to Indonesia and Southern India. Its volatile oils and curcumin, the yellow/orange pigment, have been proved to offer protection against inflammatory diseases comparable to modern drugs.

Japanese clear broth

Per serving: 112 cals 1.4g fat 0.7g sat fat 1.4g protein 17.4g carbs 0.8g fibre

This is an elegant and light soup. There are many variations in additions, from onions and different mushrooms, to adding a little more substance in the form of prawns.

Serves 4

* 1 litre/1¾ pints chicken stock
* 125 ml/4 fl oz mirin
* 1 tbsp shoyu
* 4 shiitake mushrooms, finely sliced
* 50 g/1¾ oz carrot, finely sliced
* 4 chives, each folded in half and tied in a knot
* 4 thin lemon slices

How to make it

Place the chicken stock in a large saucepan and bring to the boil.

Stir in the mirin and soy sauce, then reduce the heat and simmer for 2 minutes.

Add the mushrooms and carrot and simmer for a further 2 minutes.

Divide the soup between 4 warmed bowls and place a knotted chive and a lemon slice on top of each. Serve immediately.

Chive alive

Chives are reported to have a beneficial effect on the circulatory system and also have mild stimulant, diuretic, and antiseptic properties. Chives are also rich in vitamins A and C and are rich in calcium and iron.

Steamed mussels in lemon grass broth

Per serving: 200 cals 9.4g fat 5.4g sat fat 7.5g protein 8.1g carbs 0.6g fibre

The clean refreshing flavour of lemon grass is perfect
with richly flavoured mussels.

Serves 4

* 2 shallots, chopped
* 2 lemon grass stalks, fibrous outer leaves discarded, stems bashed with the flat of a knife
* 4 thin slices galangal or fresh ginger
* 2 garlic cloves, chopped
* 1 small tomato, chopped
* 300 ml/10 fl oz dry white wine
* 900 g/2 lb live mussels, scrubbed and debearded
* 40 g/1½ oz butter
* 2 tbsp chopped fresh coriander
* salt and pepper (optional)

Time to get started

Put the shallots, lemon grass, galangal, garlic and tomato in a large, covered wok. Pour in the wine, season to taste with salt and pepper, if using, and bring to the boil. Reduce the heat slightly and simmer for 5 minutes.

Discard any mussels with broken shells and any that refuse to close when tapped. Tip the mussels into the wok, cover and cook for 5 minutes, shaking the wok occasionally, until the mussel shells have opened. Discard any mussels that remain closed.

Drain the mussels in a colander set over a bowl. Pour the liquid into a small wok. Simmer over a low heat for a few minutes, then whisk in the butter. Taste and adjust the seasoning, if necessary.

Divide the mussels between warmed bowls.
Pour over the liquid, sprinkle with the coriander and serve immediately.

Mussel power

Mussels are low in saturated fat and high in protein, while also containing some omega-3 essential fats and a wide range of vitamins and many minerals in excellent amounts. They are also low in cholesterol and a good source of B vitamins, providing over 100 per cent of daily B12 needs.

Replenish

Chunky squash and mixed bean soup

Per serving: 302 cals   5.7g fat   1.5g sat fat   16.9g protein   52g carbs   11.8g fibre

This chunky soup is more of a main meal in a bowl. Dried beans make an easy, cheap and filling storecupboard base to any soup, and they're also rich in complex carbohydrates, B vitamins, minerals and protein and can help to lower cholesterol.

Serves 4

* 55 g/2 oz dried aduki beans
* 55 g/2 oz dried pinto beans
* 55 g/2 oz dried black turtle beans
* 1 tbsp olive oil
* 1 onion, chopped
* 2 garlic cloves, finely chopped
* 450 g/1 lb butternut squash, deseeded, peeled and diced
* 450 g/1 lb tomatoes, peeled and diced
* 1 tsp fennel seeds
* ½ tsp hot smoked paprika
* 850 ml/1½ pints vegetable stock
* 70 g/2½ oz kale, thinly shredded
* 200 g/7 oz cauliflower, cut into small florets
* 150 g/5½ oz fat-free natural Greek-style yogurt
* 1 garlic clove, finely chopped
* 2 tbsp chopped fresh basil
* salt and pepper (optional)

Meal in a bowl

Put the aduki beans, pinto beans and black turtle beans into a bowl, cover with cold water and leave to soak overnight.

Drain the soaked beans, add to a saucepan, cover with cold water and bring to the boil. Boil briskly for 10 minutes, then simmer for a further 20 minutes.

Meanwhile, heat the oil in a separate large saucepan, add the onion and fry over a medium heat, stirring, for 5 minutes until lightly coloured. Stir in the garlic, squash and tomatoes. Add the fennel seeds, paprika and stock and bring to the boil, stirring. Cover and simmer for 20 minutes.

Drain the beans and stir them into the pan of vegetables. Cover and simmer for 15 minutes. Add the kale and cauliflower, re-cover and cook for 5 minutes until just tender. Add salt and pepper to taste, if using.

Mix the yogurt with the garlic and basil. Ladle the soup into shallow warmed bowls, top with some of the garlicky yogurt and serve immediately.

Scotch broth

Per serving: 326 cals 11g fat 4.2g sat fat 25.8g protein 31.7g carbs 5.3g fibre

Bone broths are rich in minerals and contain both amino acids and gelatine. It is thought that gelatine may help heal and maintain the health of the mucosal lining of the digestive tract so that you can absorb the maximum nutrients from your food.

Serves 4

* 300 g/10½ oz lean braising steak, trimmed of all fat, cut into small dice
* 55 g/2 oz oat groats
* 225 g/8 oz carrots, cut into small dice
* 225 g/8 oz swedes, cut into small dice
* 150 g/5½ oz leeks, sliced
* 3 tbsp chopped fresh parsley
* salt (optional)

Broth

* 2 kg/4 lb 8 oz beef bones, cut into large pieces
* 2 onions, cut into chunks
* 175 g/6 oz leeks, sliced
* 225 g/8 oz carrots, thickly sliced
* 3 celery sticks, thickly sliced
* 3 litres/5¼ pints water
* 1 fresh or dried bouquet garni
* 1 tsp black peppercorns, roughly crushed

Create your soup

To make the broth, preheat the oven to 220°C/425°F/Gas Mark 7. Put the beef bones into a large roasting tin and cook in the preheated oven for 30 minutes until just beginning to brown. Turn the bones over and add the onions, leeks, carrots and celery. Roast for a further 30 minutes until the bones are a deep brown and the vegetables are tinged brown.

Scoop the bones and vegetables from the tin with a large slotted spoon, draining off as much fat as possible, and transfer to a large saucepan.

Add the water, bouquet garni and peppercorns. Bring to the boil, skimming off any foam, then cover and simmer gently for 4 hours.

Strain the broth through a muslin-lined fine sieve into a large measuring jug. You should have about 2 litres/3½ pints. Leave to cool, then chill overnight.

The next day, scoop the fat from the top of the broth and discard, then spoon the jellied stock into a saucepan and add the beef and oat groats. Bring to the boil, then simmer gently for 1 hour. Add the carrots, swedes and leeks and cook for a further 15 minutes.

Add a little salt to taste, if using, then stir in the parsley, ladle into warmed bowls and serve immediately.

Ramen with pak choi & tofu

Per serving: 359 cals   12.3g fat   2.6g sat fat   17.4g protein   50.6g carbs   5.3g fibre

This simple but richly flavoured soup makes a quick and satisfying meal. Barbecuing the pak choi and tofu adds an intriguing layer of smokiness to the dish.

Serves 4

* 350 g/12 oz extra firm tofu, cut into 2.5 cm/1 inch thick slices
* 15 g/½ oz dried shiitake mushrooms
* 1.5 litres/2¾ pints vegetable stock
* 5 tbsp soy sauce
* 1 tbsp sake or dry white wine
* 10-cm/4-inch piece fresh ginger, peeled and sliced
* 4 tbsp rice vinegar
* 4 tsp sesame oil
* 350 g/12 oz pak choi, halved or quartered lengthways
* 1 tbsp clear honey
* 225 g/8 oz fresh shiitake mushrooms
* 350 g/12 oz dried ramen noodles (flavouring sachet discarded, if included)
* 4 spring onions, thinly sliced, to garnish

Time to get started

Place the tofu slices in a single layer on a large baking tray lined with a clean tea towel. Top with another clean tea towel. Place a second baking tray on top and weigh it down with heavy dishes or cans of food to squeeze as much moisture from the tofu as possible. Set aside for 30 minutes.

Meanwhile, soak the dried mushrooms in hot water for 30 minutes. Drain, reserving the liquid, and slice the mushrooms.

Combine the stock, 4 tablespoons of the soy sauce, the sake, mushroom soaking water, ginger, 1 tablespoon of the vinegar and 1 teaspoon of the sesame oil in a medium-sized saucepan. Bring to a simmer over a medium heat. Reduce the heat to low and simmer for about 15 minutes. Remove and discard the ginger slices. Add the reserved soaked mushrooms and simmer for a further 15 minutes, or until the mushrooms are tender.

Meanwhile, preheat the barbecue or grill to medium. Place the pak choi in a microwave safe dish, cover and cook in the microwave on High for about 3 minutes. Whisk together the remaining vinegar, the remaining soy sauce, the honey and the remaining sesame oil in a large bowl. Brush the tofu all over with the sauce, then add the pak choi and fresh mushrooms to the bowl and toss to coat well. Place the tofu and vegetables on the barbecue rack and cook for about 2 minutes on each side, until nicely charred and tender. Brush with any remaining sauce. Slice the tofu into 5-cm/2-inch wide strips.

Bring the soup back to the boil. Add the noodles and cook, breaking them up with a spoon, for 3 minutes, or until tender. Stir in the spring onions. Serve immediately, topped with the tofu and vegetables.

Hot & sour soup with salmon

Per serving: 192 cals   11.2g fat   2.8g sat fat   15g protein   9.8g carbs   1.6g fibre

A classic soup to find in Chinese restaurants, this version includes salmon for a tasty twist on this well-loved dish.

Serves 4

* 225 g/8 oz skinless salmon fillet, cut into 2 or 3 pieces
* 2 tsp sesame oil
* 1 litre/1¾ pints chicken or vegetable stock
* 25 g/1 oz fresh coriander, stalks and leaves separated
* 2 bird's eye chillies, halved lengthways
* 1 lemon grass stalk, roughly chopped
* 225 g/8 oz chestnut mushrooms, quartered
* 2 tbsp nam pla (fish sauce)
* 100 g/3½ oz mangetout, diagonally sliced
* 4 spring onions, thinly sliced
* finely grated zest and juice of 2 limes

Create your soup

Preheat the grill to high. Place the salmon on a foil lined grill pan and brush lightly with the sesame oil. Grill for 3–4 minutes until just cooked through. Flake into bite-sized pieces and set aside.

Pour the stock into a large saucepan. Add the coriander stalks, chillies and lemon grass. Bring to the boil, cover and simmer for 5 minutes. Strain through a sieve into a bowl, remove and discard the flavourings and return the stock to the pan.

Add the mushrooms and nam pla to the pan. Cover and simmer for 3 minutes. Meanwhile, shred half the coriander leaves.

Add the mangetout, spring onions, shredded coriander leaves, salmon and lime zest to the pan and reheat gently. Stir in the lime juice to taste. Ladle into warmed bowls, sprinkle with the remaining coriander leaves and serve immediately.

Simple salmon

Fish oils in salmon help to keep the skin smooth, can help beat eczema and also prevent dry eyes. It is also known to help minimize joint pain and arthritis and may reduce the risk of some cancers and protect against stroke.

Jerk turkey soup

Per serving: 239 cals 6.4g fat 1.2g sat fat 22.5g protein 23.9g carbs 4.7g fibre

This soup has all the flavour of Jamaican jerk spices and seasoning and uses ground spices from the storecupboard, plus a can of cooked black-eyed beans, fresh tomatoes and low-fat turkey breast, to make a filling and reviving soup.

Serves 4

* 1 tbsp olive oil
* 1 onion, finely chopped
* 2 garlic cloves, finely chopped
* 2-cm/¾-inch piece fresh ginger, peeled and finely chopped
* ¼ tsp grated nutmeg
* ½ tsp ground allspice
* ½ tsp dried crushed red chillies
* 2 tsp ground cumin
* 2 tsp fresh thyme leaves
* 450 g/1 lb tomatoes, peeled and roughly chopped
* 600 ml/1 pint turkey stock
* 1 tbsp tomato purée
* 1 tbsp dark muscovado sugar
* 400 g/14 oz canned black-eyed beans in water, drained
* 280 g/10 oz turkey breast fillet portions
* 2 tbsp chopped fresh coriander
* salt and pepper (optional)

How to make it

Heat the oil in a saucepan over a medium heat, add the onion and fry, stirring, for 5 minutes until just beginning to colour. Sprinkle over the garlic and ginger, then add the nutmeg, allspice, chillies and cumin. Add the thyme and tomatoes and mix together well.

Pour in the stock, add the tomato purée, sugar, beans and turkey pieces and bring to the boil. Cover and simmer for 30 minutes or until the turkey pieces are cooked through with no hint of pink juices when pierced in the thickest parts with a knife. Lift the turkey pieces out of the pan, transfer to a plate and tear into shreds with two forks.

Stir the coriander into the soup with salt and pepper to taste, if using. Ladle into warmed bowls, then top with the shreds of turkey and serve immediately.

Get to the root of it

The main active compounds in ginger are terpenes and gingerols, which have anti-cancer properties and have been shown to destroy colon, ovarian and rectal cancer cells.

Vegetable goulash soup

Per serving: 137 cals 6g fat 1.3g sat fat 3.3g protein 20.7g carbs 5.2g fibre

There's no hard and fast rule to the vegetables included in this goulash soup, so feel free to either use your favourite or what's in season.

Serves 6

* 2 tbsp olive oil
* 1 large onion, chopped
* 2 garlic cloves, finely chopped
* 3–4 carrots, thinly sliced
* ½ head of Savoy cabbage, cored and shredded
* 1 small red pepper, deseeded and chopped
* 1 tbsp plain flour
* 2 tbsp sweet paprika
* 1 litre/1¾ pints vegetable stock
* 2 potatoes, cut into chunks
* 1–2 tsp sugar (optional)
* salt and pepper (optional)

Meal in a bowl

Heat the oil in a large saucepan. Add the onion, garlic and carrots and cook over a low heat, stirring occasionally, for 8–10 minutes, until lightly coloured. Add the cabbage and red pepper and cook, stirring frequently, for 3–4 minutes.

Sprinkle in the flour and paprika, and cook, stirring constantly, for 1 minute. Gradually stir in the stock, a little at a time. Increase the heat to medium and bring to the boil, stirring constantly. Season to taste with salt and pepper, if using, then reduce the heat, cover and simmer for 30 minutes.

Add the potatoes and bring back to the boil, then reduce the heat, re-cover the pan and simmer for a further 20–30 minutes, until the potatoes are soft but not falling apart.

Taste and adjust the seasoning, if necessary and stir in the sugar, if using. Ladle the soup into warmed bowls and serve immediately.

Pepper power

All peppers are rich in vitamins A, C and K, but red peppers are simply bursting with them. Antioxidant vitamins A and C help to prevent cell damage, cancer and diseases related to ageing, and they support immune function. They also reduce inflammation such as that found in arthritis and asthma.

Chargrilled aubergine with lamb & minted pomegranate soup

Per serving: 318 cals 14.4g fat 4.9g sat fat 22g protein 31.1g carbs 9.8g fibre

Spoon down through the layers for a real taste sensation. Bite through the fruity jewel-like pomegranate seeds to fresh tangy mint, then wonderfully smoky aubergine, then on to a layer of spinach followed by a garlicky Middle-Eastern lamb broth below.

Serves 4

* 1 tbsp olive oil
* 550 g/1 lb 4 oz lamb foreshanks on the bone
* 1 onion, finely chopped
* 2 garlic cloves, finely chopped
* 350 g/12 oz tomatoes, peeled and roughly chopped
* 1 tsp ground cumin
* 1 tsp ground coriander
* ½ tsp turmeric
* 850 ml/1½ pints lamb stock
* 55 g/2 oz wheat berries
* 2 aubergines, 600 g/1 lb 5 oz total weight
* juice of ½ lemon
* 200 g/7 oz baby spinach, rinsed and drained
* 2 tbsp chopped fresh mint
* 50 g/1¾ oz pomegranate seeds
* salt and pepper (optional)

Time to get started

Heat the oil in a saucepan, add the lamb and onion and fry over a medium heat for 5 minutes, turning the lamb and stirring the onion until both are lightly browned.

Add the garlic and tomatoes to the pan, then sprinkle over the cumin, coriander and turmeric. Pour in the stock, bring to the boil, then reduce the heat, cover and simmer for 1 hour. Add the wheat berries to the soup and cook for a further 30 minutes until the wheat berries are tender and the lamb is almost falling off the bone.

Meanwhile, preheat the grill to high and line a grill pan with foil. Prick the aubergines two or three times at the base, place in the prepared pan and grill for 20–25 minutes, turning occasionally, until blackened and charred all over.

Lift the lamb out of the soup and transfer to a plate, then remove the meat with two forks, discarding the bones and any fat. Keep the meat warm. Add the lemon juice to the soup with salt and pepper to taste, if using.

Add the spinach and any water still clinging to the leaves to a large frying pan and cook over a medium heat for 2 minutes until just wilted. Break away some of the charred aubergine skin, then scoop out the soft flesh from inside and roughly chop, discarding the remaining skin.

Divide the lamb between four heatproof glass tumblers. Ladle the soup into the tumblers, top each with a layer of spinach, spoonfuls of the aubergine, the chopped mint and the pomegranate seeds, then serve immediately.

French onion soup

Per serving: 433 cals 25.8g fat 11.9g sat fat 19.9g protein 31g carbs 2.7g fibre

For a naughty little twist to this French classic, add 2 tablespoons of brandy to the soup just before serving.

Serves 6

* 3 tbsp olive oil
* 675 g/1 lb 8 oz onions, thinly sliced
* 4 garlic cloves, 3 chopped and 1 halved
* 1 tsp sugar
* 2 tsp chopped fresh thyme, plus 6 extra sprigs to garnish
* 2 tbsp plain flour
* 125 ml/4 fl oz dry white wine
* 2 litres/3½ pints vegetable stock
* 6 slices French bread
* 300 g/10½ oz Gruyère cheese, grated

Create your soup

Heat the oil in a large, heavy-based saucepan over a medium-low heat, add the onions and cook, stirring occasionally, for 10 minutes, or until they are just beginning to brown. Stir in the chopped garlic, sugar and chopped thyme, then reduce the heat and cook, stirring occasionally, for 30 minutes, or until the onions are golden brown.

Sprinkle in the flour and cook, stirring constantly, for 1–2 minutes. Stir in the wine. Gradually stir in the stock and bring to the boil, skimming off any scum that rises to the surface, then reduce the heat and simmer for 45 minutes.

Meanwhile, preheat the grill to medium. Toast the bread on both sides under the grill, then rub the toast with the cut edges of the halved garlic clove.

Ladle the soup into 6 flameproof bowls set on a baking tray. Float a piece of toast in each bowl and divide the grated cheese between them. Place under the grill for 2–3 minutes, or until the cheese has just melted. Garnish with thyme sprigs and serve immediately.

Need a little thyme

The evergreen leaves of thyme have a powerful, aromatic flavour and strong antioxidant action because of the volatile oils and plant compounds they contain. The most important of these is thymol oil that boost the effects of healthy omega-3 fats on the body, which have been shown to be important for healthy brain function.

Saffron & prawn broth

Per serving: 61 cals 0.7g fat 0.1g sat fat 6.3g protein 7.6g carbs 0.4g fibre

Don't be put off by the idea of making your own fish soup, it is really very easy and if you chat to your fishmonger the day before you plan to make the soup he will reserve some trimmings and bones for you, and may not even charge you for them.

Serves 4

* 200 g/7 oz large raw tiger prawns heads, tails and shells intact
* 1 kg/2 lb 4 oz fish trimmings, bones and heads
* 1 onion, roughly chopped
* 115 g/4 oz carrots, sliced
* 250 g/9 oz fennel, chopped
* 3 tomatoes, roughly chopped
* pared rind and juice of 1 lemon
* 150 ml/5 fl oz dry white wine
* 1 litre/1¾ pints water
* 2 large pinches of saffron threads
* ½ tsp white peppercorns, roughly crushed
* salt (optional)
* 1 tomato, deseeded and finely diced, to garnish

How to make it

Remove the prawn heads and tails and reserve, then peel away the shell and devein. Chill and reserve the peeled prawns. Add the fish trimmings, bones and heads to a large saucepan with the other prawn trimmings.

Add the onion, carrots, fennel, tomatoes and lemon rind to the pan. Pour in the wine and water, then add 1 pinch of the saffron threads and the peppercorns.

Bring to the boil, cover and simmer gently for 30 minutes. Strain through a fine sieve into a large measuring jug. You should have about 1.2 litre/2 pints. Pour the strained liquid into a clean saucepan. If you have too much broth, boil rapidly to reduce it and concentrate the flavours.

Add the reserved prawns and the remaining saffron. Cook gently for 2–3 minutes until the prawns are bright pink. Taste the broth and add salt, if using, then add the lemon juice.

Ladle the broth into warmed bowls, add the prawns, then garnish with the diced tomato and serve immediately.

Ribollita

Per serving: 484 cals   18.8g fat   4g sat fat   16g protein   67.4g carbs   15.2g fibre

Originating from Italy, this beautiful soup uses an abundance of colourful, delicious vegetables to create a soup to satisfy.

Serves 4

* 400 g/14 oz canned haricot or cannellini beans, drained and rinsed
* 3 tbsp olive oil, plus extra for drizzling
* 1 Spanish onion, chopped
* 1 leek, chopped
* 4 garlic cloves, finely chopped
* 2 carrots, diced
* 2 celery sticks, chopped
* 2 potatoes, diced
* 2 courgettes, diced
* 2 large tomatoes, peeled, deseeded and chopped
* 1 tsp sun-dried tomato paste
* 1 dried chilli, crushed (optional)
* 1.7 litres/3 pints vegetable stock
* 225 g/8 oz cavolo nero, cored and shredded
* 225 g/8 oz Savoy cabbage, cored and shredded
* salt and pepper (optional)

Croûtes

* 4 slices of ciabatta
* 2 garlic cloves, halved

Meal in a bowl

Put half the beans into a food processor or blender and process briefly to a coarse purée. Scrape into a bowl and set aside.

Heat the oil in a large saucepan. Add the onion, leek, garlic, carrots and celery and cook over a low heat, stirring occasionally, for 8–10 minutes. Add the potatoes and courgettes and cook, stirring constantly, for 2 minutes.

Add the tomatoes, sun-dried tomato paste and dried chilli, if using, and cook, stirring constantly, for 3 minutes, then stir in the bean purée. Cook, stirring constantly, for a further 2 minutes.

Pour in the stock and add the cavolo nero and Savoy cabbage. Bring to the boil, reduce the heat and simmer for 2 hours.

Towards the end of the cooking time, make the croûtes. Preheat the grill. Rub the bread with the halved garlic cloves and toast on both sides.

Stir the remaining beans into the soup and heat through gently for 10 minutes. Season to taste with salt and pepper, if using. Put a croûte in the base of each warmed bowl and ladle the soup over the top. Drizzle with a little oil and serve immediately.

Miso fish soup

Per serving: 136 cals   3.1g fat   1.3g sat fat   11.1g protein   17.6g carbs   2.4g fibre

This is a lovely light and fragrant soup, perfect as a lunch or as a starter course.

Serves 4

* 850 ml/1½ pints fish stock or vegetable stock
* 2.5-cm/1-inch piece fresh ginger, peeled and grated
* 1 tbsp nam pla (fish sauce)
* 1 fresh chilli, deseeded and finely sliced
* 1 carrot, thinly sliced
* 55 g/2 oz daikon, cut into thin strips or ½ bunch radishes, trimmed and sliced
* 1 yellow pepper, deseeded and cut into thin strips
* 85 g/3 oz shiitake mushrooms, sliced if large
* 40 g/1½ oz thread egg noodles
* 225 g/8 oz sole fillets, skinned and cut into strips
* 1 tbsp miso paste
* 4 spring onions, trimmed and shredded

To make this soup

Pour the stock into a large saucepan and add the ginger, nam pla and chilli. Bring to the boil then reduce the heat and simmer for 5 minutes.

Add the carrot with the daikon, pepper, mushrooms and noodles and simmer for a further 3 minutes.

Add the fish strips with the miso paste and continue to cook for 2 minutes, or until the fish is tender. Divide equally between warmed bowls, top with the spring onions and serve immediately.

Glorious ginger

Ginger has been proven to be as effective as prescription medicine in beating motion sickness without drowsiness. It also has proven relief from the pain of arthritis and is a great digestive aid.

Index